Praise for
Trekking toward Tenacity

"Chris offers us a unique gift in *Trekking toward Tenacity*: part Bible study, part meditation, part training for parents in how to form and shape the faith of their children. Many books do one or two of those well, but Chris skillfully leads the reader through all of them for those of us raising kids to take our own spiritual formation seriously and grow in how we walk spiritually with our kids. This book is all about how to practically learn to live in God's loving presence, putting both our spiritual and mental health front and center. Using Psalm 139 as a guide, Chris walks us directly into the intersections of our life and helps us recover how to experience God's presence, build mental and spiritual resiliency, and curate conversations with our kids about their lives and faith. If you're looking to strengthen your faith or gain a more creative imagination for how to shepherd your kids, this is a fantastic resource."
—**Matt Tebbe,** coauthor of *Having the Mind of Christ*, pastor at
The Table Indianapolis

"A wise and wonderful walk through Psalm 139, *Trekking toward Tenacity* is the kind of book you'll want to read slowly, marking it up and letting it soak deep into your heart and soul. Both conversational and honest in his style, Chris weaves Scripture and spiritual wisdom throughout this warm and gentle book. I came away thinking this: *We are all disheveled souls, but God still loves us and there is always hope.*"
—**Susy Flory,** *New York Times* bestselling author and coauthor, director of West Coast Christian Writers, and doctoral candidate at Houston Theological Seminary

"This book has the potential to save lives and build healthy dynamics in homes across the nation. Chris Morris's vulnerability about his own life and family is inspiring and a testimony of God's relentless pursuit of his children. As a pastor's wife, I hear how mental illness is affecting our families, and *Trekking toward Tenacity* is a tool I recommend to all Christian parents. It is the real deal!"
—**Jessica Taylor,** coauthor of *Pastors' Wives Tell All* and cohost of the *Pastors' Wives Tell All* podcast

"With anxiety and depression on the rise among children and teenagers, Chris Morris's insight and strategies for combating the lies and misconceptions surrounding mental health are exactly what parents need in their parenting arsenals. *Trekking toward Tenacity* provides parents with thoughtful discussion starters, enlightening Scripture explorations, and actionable steps to bettering the mental health of the whole family. As someone who serves in youth ministry and sees the debilitating effects of mental illness among our teens, I recommend this book to any Christian parent who values the mental health of their children."
—**Stephanie Gilbert,** coauthor of *Pastors' Wives Tell All* and cohost of the *Pastors' Wives Tell All* podcast

"God's Word can teach you how to parent through mental health battles. *Trekking toward Tenacity* opens your eyes to the power of Scripture, self-reflection, and activation exercises that promote healthy change and breakthrough. Our world is saturated with new mental-health cases daily. Chris focuses on pivotal points like understanding God's intimate knowledge and presence, learning gratitude, the significance of prayer, and the ability to embrace our emotions and vulnerabilities as strengths. What if learning those pivotal points would bring more peace to your home?"
—**Christy Boulware,** author of *Nervous Breakthrough*, Founder of Fearless Unite, podcast host of *Fearless Tips and Talks*

TREKKING
YOUR FAMILY'S ROADMAP
TOWARD
TO STRONGER MENTAL HEALTH
TENACITY

CHRIS MORRIS

LEAFWOOD
PUBLISHERS
an imprint of Abilene Christian University Press

TREKKING TOWARD TENACITY
Your Family's Roadmap to Stronger Mental Health

LEAFWOOD
PUBLISHERS
an imprint of *Abilene Christian University Press*

Copyright © 2024 by Chris Morris

ISBN 978-1-68426-389-9 | LCCN 2023049840

Printed in the United States of America

ALL RIGHTS RESERVED
No part of this publication may be reproduced, stored in a retrieval system, or transmitted in any form by any means—electronic, mechanical, photocopying, recording, or otherwise—without prior written consent.

All scripture quotations, unless otherwise noted, are taken from the Holy Bible, New Living Translation, copyright © 1996, 2004, 2015 by Tyndale House Foundation. Used by permission of Tyndale House Publishers, Inc., Carol Stream, Illinois 60188. All rights reserved.

Scripture quotations noted NIV are from the Holy Bible, New International Version®, NIV®, copyright © 1973, 1978, 1984, 2011 by Biblica, Inc. Used by permission. All rights reserved.

Scripture quotations noted *The Message* are taken from *The Message*, copyright © 1993, 2002, 2018 by Eugene H. Peterson. Used by permission of NavPress. All rights reserved. Represented by Tyndale House Publishers.

Published in association with Mary DeMuth Literary, mary@marydemuthliterary.com.

LIBRARY OF CONGRESS CATALOGING-IN-PUBLICATION DATA
Names: Morris, Chris, 1977-, author.
Title: Trekking toward tenacity : your family's roadmap to stronger mental health / Chris Morris.
Description: Abilene : Leafwood Publishers, 2024.
Identifiers: LCCN 2023049840 | ISBN 9781684263899 (paperback) | ISBN 9781684268665 (ebook)
Subjects: LCSH: Parenting—Religious aspects—Christianity. | Resilience (Personality trait)—
    Religious aspects—Christianity. | Families—Religious life.
Classification: LCC BV4529 .M648 2024 | DDC 248.8/45—dc23/eng/20240507
LC record available at https://lccn.loc.gov/2023049840

Cover design by Greg Jackson, Thinkpen Design
Interior text design by Sandy Armstrong, Strong Design

Leafwood Publishers is an imprint of Abilene Christian University Press.
ACU Box 29138
Abilene, Texas 79699

1-877-816-4455
www.leafwoodpublishers.com

24 25 26 27 28 29 30 // 7 6 5 4 3 2 1

For Cynthia, the toughest girl I know

CONTENTS

Introduction 9

1   God Knows Us Intimately and Still Wants to Be around Us 17
2   God Is Paying Attention to Us.. 29
3   God Sees Us 43
4   God Knows Our Words... 55
5   God Is All around and within Us... 69
6   We Must Develop a Ritual of Gratitude 81
7   We Cannot Escape God.. 93
8   Darkness Is Light to God.. 105
9   God Knows Our Broken Parts and Still Loves Us 117
10 We Are Extraordinary... 127
11 God Knows All Our Days... 137
12 We Can Be Emotional.. 151
13 We Can Pray Bravely.. 165

Conclusion 177
Acknowledgments 191

INTRODUCTION

If you've picked up this book, it's likely because either the phrase "stronger mental health" or the word "tenacity" caught your eye, and you thought that maybe you could use a bit more of one or the other in your family. I'd hazard a guess that you might be right, because I don't believe anyone ever arrives at a full tank in either tenacity or being mentally healthy. But before we go even one step further, let's take the time to define these terms, because I mean something very specific by both *stronger mental health* and *tenacity*.

What Is Tenacity?

I'd like to start with tenacity because I think the word tenacity is more often misunderstood. Too often, we think of tenacity as being tough, that person who pushes through everything life throws at them and keeps on trudging forward. We might say that synonyms for *tenacious* are "hardy" and "durable." Perhaps you envision a Marine, a hardened veteran who has seen the terrors of war but has pushed on anyway. If we were defining tenacity simply as toughness, I'll tell you whom I'd imagine: my daughter Cynthia.

You wouldn't picture Cynthia on a battlefield in a war. This isn't a commentary on whether women belong on the battlefield either; she just doesn't have the right spirit for war. You might more easily imagine any of her three brothers there, but Cynthia is by far the toughest of our kids. Her inborn toughness has been tempered through her life experiences. Cynthia is autistic and has had to fight for every victory she's experienced in her life. Nothing has come easy for her. When Cynthia was about three years old, we woke up to her screaming in the middle of the night. When we went to check on her, Cynthia had fallen out of bed and onto the tile floor. We helped her back into bed, calmed her down, and didn't think anything of it, just an unlucky fall that's bound to happen to every kid at least once. I should mention to you that, at this point, Cynthia was nonverbal.

However, we noticed about three days later that she was using her left arm to support her right arm and wouldn't use her right arm at all. We asked her if it hurt, but she couldn't give us a meaningful answer using her sign language cues, largely because both arms were occupied. We took her to urgent care and explained that we thought Cynthia had hurt her shoulder from falling out of bed several days before. The doctor didn't believe us, because Cynthia was showing no signs of distress except for supporting her right arm, but he eventually agreed to have an X-ray done to appease us. Several hours passed and the X-ray results came back—Cynthia had a hairline fracture in her right shoulder. My daughter had been walking around with a busted clavicle for three days and just gutting it out. As I said, she's the toughest in my family.

However, this kind of grinding-it-out toughness is not what I mean when I use the word *tenacity*. Let me give you a different word picture to help encapsulate the idea I have in my mind for tenacity. Imagine a tree in the middle of a severe wind storm. Its branches whip around, its leaves are torn from it, pieces of its bark rip off, and the trunk of the tree bends under the strength of the wind it's facing, but the tree stands firm in the chaos because it has deep roots. This is tenacity—standing strong in the whirlwind of life and holding firmly to our convictions because of the root system we've established in our lives.

As Christians, one of the core roots we should have can be found in the goodness of God. Hebrews 11:6 puts it this way: "It is impossible to please God without faith. Anyone who wants to come to him must believe that God exists and that he rewards those who sincerely seek him." Even when a storm swirls about our lives and brings havoc, we stay rooted in the idea that God is good and he rewards those who seek him. But establishing roots like this in our own lives is no easy task, much less in the lives of our children. Together, we will explore what this means for us today.

What Does It Mean to Have Stronger Mental Health?

A tree's root system is my image of tenacity, but what about having stronger mental health? Let's again start with what I don't mean. I don't mean having a family without any mental health conditions. That's not fair, because nobody chooses to have mental health problems, and we shouldn't say that somebody with a mental health condition cannot develop a mentally healthy outlook on life.

It's time to get real with you. I have major depressive disorder. I've been in the mental health ward more than once, and I have survived a suicide attempt. All of these are facts about me; but here's another fact equally true about me: I am stronger mentally than I have been in decades, perhaps ever. I have taken steps that have paved the way for me to arrive at a space where I am mentally healthy, despite my diagnosis. I have learned to have increased emotional self-awareness, so I know when something is "off" with me. I have learned how to be transparent with my inner circle when I start to struggle with depression again. I have refused to allow my diagnosis to define the whole of my being. These tools, along with others like counseling and medication, have allowed me to thrive despite my diagnosis.

Being mentally strong isn't about having or not having a mental-health diagnosis though. I believe it's easy to be mentally unhealthy without having a mental-health diagnosis. Being mentally strong means being able to stay the course when life gets rocky. It means having the tool kit, the experience, the interpersonal support, and the capacity to maintain the trajectory of your life when the bottom falls out. A person without a mental-health condition can be mentally weaker in this area than a person with one.

Helping Our Children Become Stronger Mentally

This again raises the question: How can we help our children be mentally strong individuals, and what can we do as parents to give them the best chance to maintain a steady trajectory in life when the bottom falls out? I believe the only path to a steady course in life is found in the pages of the Bible. Many other tools are incredibly valuable. I don't mean to insinuate in any way that (for example) counseling and medication aren't sometimes necessary to find mental stability, and I use any number of tools in my own life to maintain my sense of mental strength, but I am also confident that any other foundation is bound to disappoint in the end. I use the word *foundation* on purpose here. Let's use mindfulness as an example. Mindfulness on its own will only get us so far in managing our emotions, but if we combine mindfulness alongside intimacy with the Holy Spirit, then we will get much further. Knowing the heart of God is the foundation for all other tools or habits we can develop to establish mentally strong approaches to life.

Introduction

The pages of this book are based on a beautiful passage of Scripture: Psalm 139. In this psalm, we can see David declaring any number of powerful things about God. Beyond that, though, he declares things that are true about himself, and consequently about us and our children. The psalm clearly tells of God's intimate knowledge of us, with all our warts and all our challenges and all our disappointing decisions. Despite all these things, God loves us. Period. End of story. God has nothing but affection for us as his children, regardless of how messed up we might be right now. God knows us intimately and still wants to be around us. Not only that, but God's affection is also not some absentee type of affection, where God loves us from afar. No, God pays attention to us and still adores us.

There's a powerful corollary to God paying attention to us in that we aren't left to our own devices. God isn't a deistic God, one who wound up the gigantic clock of the universe to set everything in motion and then walked away to do something more important. When we have great things happen in our lives, God rejoices with us. When we find ourselves at our worst, God weeps right alongside us. We can rest assured that God will not condemn us but will instead bring strong love and a broken heart for our pain.

Psalm 139:5 has one of the most beautiful images in all of Scripture hidden in it. This verse says God goes before us, walks behind us, and is upon us. New Testament theology would add that the Holy Spirit dwells within us. Taken together, we are quite literally surrounded by God in all our circumstances. God goes before us, weaving peace and his presence into situations. God follows behind with his grace, forgiving all our mistakes. God is upon us, providing his intimate guidance and support through any difficulties we might face. When we walk forward to the New Testament, Jesus says in John 14 that he will not leave us as orphans in this world. This promise is fulfilled by the indwelling of the Holy

Sprit. Now, God is within us and is committed to staying with us regardless of what may come.

That last paragraph was a preview of what you will find in this book. I will break down each verse or series of verses, drawing application points along the way. There will also be stories of people—myself and others—who have found hope in God in their daily lives, their victories, and their struggles. I will include some exegesis of the words found in Scripture, but the emphasis in this book will be on finding the best applications of what we read for our everyday lives. Even more specifically, this book will emphasize how we can turn these beautiful ideas from the Bible into practical parenting concepts that will empower our children to be both resilient and mentally healthy.

I am convinced the Bible can help us and our children understand how to cope with the inevitable stressors that life brings. The Word of God can teach us who we are, remind us what our limits are, and even give us examples of how different people have dealt with circumstances in their lives. We can also learn how to meaningfully contribute to the lives of others around us. Taken together, these elements allow us as families to step into stronger mental health. Not all the ideas listed in every chapter will apply to your family, because each family is unique. For example, my daughter is autistic, so we have had to adjust our own uses of ideas like these to accommodate her unique abilities. The key is to be intentional about building habits of mental strength into your kids' lives in a way that fits how they function.

What to Expect in This Book

Each chapter in this book will follow the same format. The chapter will open with the verse or verses from Psalm 139 that we will be exploring together. We will then enter into the "Engaging with the

Bible" section, which will be a combination of questions, stories, and examples to help us understand what the passage means.

From there, we will move to a section labeled "Engaging Our Kids with This Truth," where the big idea of each section of Psalm 139 will be applied to our parenting. Most chapters will have different applications for different age groups, because talking to a kindergartener differs from talking to a teenager.

Next comes the "Engaging with Yourself" section. This will comprise several reflection questions, where you can consider the main message of the chapter and how it applies to you. The chapters will end with a "Verse to Consider or Memorize" that relates to the key message of the chapter. Sometimes the verse will be from Psalm 139, and sometimes it will come from elsewhere in Scripture. I hope it will be a source of encouragement and strength for you in your parenting journey. We will discuss briefly what this verse means for our parenting and how we can coach our children to apply the verse in their lives.

My prayer for you as you continue reading this book is threefold. First, I want you to be encouraged in your parenting, to discover that there is no magical formula to perfect parenting; we all just do our best with the tools we have at any given moment. Second, I want you to find strength in the numerous practices that are outlined in this book so you don't feel alone in the parenting journey. Third, I want you to have greater hope for your children to become mentally stronger and more tenacious in Christ.

1

GOD KNOWS US INTIMATELY AND STILL WANTS TO BE AROUND US

*"O Lord, you have examined my heart
and know everything about me."*
Psalm 139:1

Engaging the Bible

Oh Dear, He Knows Everything
When we read that God has examined our hearts and knows everything, this might induce a sense of dread. We could be filled with fear. God knows all the grossness and yuck that exists inside our hearts. How could God want anything to do with us? Most of us are disheveled souls trying to find our way through a challenging world as best we can with our faith intact, and it's often tough sledding to do so. If we're being brutally honest with ourselves, we probably don't like every corner of our hearts the same, and

we aren't a holy God who demands perfection from his followers. What a terrifying thought to have our spirits laid bare before God!

It's even more disconcerting when we think about bringing our parental responsibilities before the Lord. Nobody has all their stuff together every part of the day as a parent, and we all have bad moments, bad days, or even bad seasons. We've all had times when we've blown up at our kids when they've honestly done nothing wrong; we were just stressed about something else and took it out on them. And then there are the seasons in our lives that feel overwhelmingly crazy because of schedules and habits and all the to-do lists. For months on end, we're getting out of bed just in time to arrive for work, if we're not late, and by the time our workday ends, we find ourselves exhausted. Making dinner isn't even an option, so we stop and get takeout, again. Then we plop in front of the television and zone out for a few hours before heading to bed, unless the kids have activities those evenings, which it seems like they always do. Then we're rushing them to the soccer field or the church campus or the karate lesson or their friend's house for a sleepover. There's no room for homework support, no room for helping with social problems, and no room for conversations about God or discipleship. There's no room for anything because we're already operating at about 120 percent capacity for all our waking hours.

Whenever we stop to consider this, we might be overcome with shame. We know God wants more for us and more from us and that we're lying down on the job because we have no spare energy for anything other than what we're already managing. So we do our best to ignore the growing sense of guilt that gnaws at the back of our minds and to keep going as best we can, knowing in our heart of hearts it's not good enough. How can the God who created the heavens and the earth want anything to do with someone like that, who's subsisting, barely? God can't and shouldn't want to engage us at all, we might think to ourselves, because God is holy and we're a mess.

And we know we're not the only ones God is interested in, not the only ones God knows intimately. There are also our children, the ones we barely have time to engage with between work and activities and dinner and relaxing and sleeping (let's not forget sleeping again). God intimately knows all the challenges they're going through, all the challenges of peer pressure and social media. God knows that they often feel alone in this world that gets bigger every day, and God also knows that we're not helping make it more manageable a lot of the days. Our kids are known by God too, and what if God is already judging them like he might be judging us? What if our kids are being set up to be the same type of spiritual almost-failures that we are because we're not investing enough time in them?

Let's Flip the Script

That's a pretty disheartening scene, isn't it? But what if the message of Psalm 139:1 isn't one of condemnation at all? What if we had it wrong the whole time? Bear with me for a moment while I tease out a different reaction we might have to the idea that God knows all our junk. There can be a sense of relief that floods into our hearts at the idea of God already knowing everything going on within us. It removes the fear of future rejection. Think back to when you were dating for a moment. There's a push and pull between keeping your best foot forward and letting that person see the *real you*. If you let the *real you* out too soon, you think they might bolt in utter terror. On the flip side, if you never let the *real you* out, then they will never know who you are.

So both of you begin a bit of a dance, a bit of a show-and-tell session, where you slowly uncover different aspects of yourself to each other, hoping the interest doesn't wane. I remember this stage with my now-wife, and it was stressful every time a weird little fact about my life came out. I remember wondering several times if she would stop being interested in me because I was too weird or too broken for her.

Here's something oddly specific I remember worrying about: my fandom of all things Star Trek. Mind you, I'm not the guy who dresses up as a Vulcan with pointy ears and goes to conventions hoping to meet the cast of the original Star Trek television show, but I know a thing or twelve about the show. I've seen most of the episodes several times, and I have been known to quote characters from the show without warning. So I was worried she would slink away if she ever found this out about me. I almost actively hid it from her, even avoiding opportunities to talk about the show or the movies when they unusually came up in conversation. Eventually, the cat came out of the bag. I don't remember the specific moment any longer, but one day it happened. And then I found out something weirdly wonderful about Barbara: she loves Star Trek too. She preferred the newer series, but she nerded out with me over the show.

So all my anxiety about this specific element of who I am was completely unneeded. We had a weird thing in common and didn't even know it! Over twenty-five years of marriage later, she's still by my side with all the weirdness and brokenness. And now that we've reached the stage where there aren't any secrets between us, it brings relief to me. I don't have to worry about her running because of some new fact. She knows all the facts, and she's still committed to me and our relationship.

No Secrets with God
This same sense of relief can flood over us when we realize God knows us intimately and has yet to give up on us. Does God know

I like Star Trek and still want to be around me? Yes. Obviously, I'm using a silly example to make a serious point about God's commitment to us. Like my wife and me, there are no secrets between us and God, and he's not running away. Nothing will change God's commitment to being with us. What a truly remarkable fact, given God's perfection and our imperfections. And yet God stays, loving us and staying committed to our relationship. Even more stunning, God knows the ins and outs, the ups and downs, the down and out times of our family and is still for us.

It can be hard to imagine that God is so thoroughly on our side, but the Scriptures burst at the seams with this fact. My favorite example is Romans 8:31: "If God is for us, who can ever be against us?" It's such a straightforward assessment of how God feels about us. God is for us. If we are battling that sense of overwhelm we talked about earlier, it's okay—God is for us. If we are struggling to find time to engage meaningfully with our children regularly, it's okay—God is for us. If we are even deep in the pits of despair and depression, it's okay—God is for us. If our anxiety is making it hard for us to function in our daily lives, it's okay—God is for us.

This revolutionary truth can bring so much freedom to our souls and can have a dramatic impact on the way we parent. No longer do we have to be bound up in insecurity around our capabilities, because God is for us. It's not necessary for us to second-guess every step we take, because God is for us. Now look, I understand that having God on our side doesn't solve every problem. In one sense, nothing has changed. And yet in another, everything has changed. Knowing that we have the ongoing support of the creator of heaven and earth should change the way we view our family interactions.

Engaging Our Kids with This Truth

I promised you this wasn't a theology book but a parenting book, so let's get to work on the most important question we can ask based on the ideas in this chapter: How can we help our kids understand that God knows them intimately and still wants to be around them? What can we do practically to engage with our children and teach them that God is for them? This might surprise you, but there isn't a magic formula or a specific conversation you can have one time with your kids that will establish for them a foundation of trust in God. It just doesn't work that way. Instead, it's a process that takes time, repetition, diligence, and care. But it's important to initiate this practice as soon as you can, because our children will develop tenacity as a direct result of understanding that God is intimately acquainted with every aspect of their lives.

It starts by committing to a mild simplification of your life and your calendar. The bottom line is, you cannot communicate anything of spiritual value to your children if you never engage them in spiritual conversations, and that won't ever happen if there's no time or energy left in the days to talk at all. I get it, we all have busy lives—work is demanding, your kids like karate lessons, you like your television shows, and it's nice to just relax once in a while. Something must give, though, if you want to raise resilient and mentally healthy kids. I'm not talking here about quitting your job and killing your social life. On the contrary, my suggestion is to set aside a consistent night on a regular basis to talk together about whatever comes up.

If your schedule allows, it's best to do this on the same night every week because consistency breeds anticipation. But if you can't do it every week or on the same day, that's fine—just prioritize regular open-ended conversation time with your kids. The anticipation can still be built simply by reminding your kids that it's coming up and to be ready to ask and answer some questions.

It's been our experience with our kids that they have grown to enjoy these times immensely, and they do look forward to the time now. At first, it was a hard sell, I'm not going to lie. "We are just going to talk, but about what? There's nothing to talk about," they'd say. But we pushed forward with our planned conversations, and everything flowed naturally, to be honest. There was sharing, communication of love, and trust given and received. It was a win, and it still is even though most of our kids don't live at home any longer. We now have pathways for more spiritual conversations because we were open to whatever topics our kids wanted to discuss.

Not a Bible Study but a Connection Time
I'm not necessarily talking here about a family Bible study. If you want to include that as part of your time together, go for it. I'm sure that could be meaningful if done consistently and well. I'll be honest and tell you that we haven't done regular Bible studies in a while at my house because the kids aren't that interested and I don't want to die on that hill. The goal here isn't to teach our kids the best theology available to them but to carve out a specific time regularly to connect about whatever is happening in life. I *will* die on the hill of regular, planned connection time with my kids.

In these moments, we can ask the typical questions about school and friends and also the atypical questions about how God fits into their daily lives. It's in these moments that we learn when our kids are struggling with something they don't want to talk about, and it's here when they trust us with hard things. If they choose not to share with us, we give them grace and privacy instead of forcing the issue. Instead, we ask them to consider talking with us in the future when they are comfortable doing so.

Whenever they do share hard things with us, we can reflect the unchanging love of God to our children. It's been said that the first view kids have of God is through their parents, so we should take this opportunity to step into the proverbial shoes of God and demonstrate exactly who God is. No matter what the issue is, we should respond with love and acceptance. It's easier said than done because our kids might end up in deep waters with breaking the law or sexual issues or radical dishonesty, and we might not agree with the decisions they've made. But now isn't the time to bring up the "right decisions" to make—now we must love them unconditionally. We can address morality later, but first, we must settle their hearts.

Whether our child is seven and scared about stealing a piece of candy from the corner store or our child is sixteen and wondering whether they might be transgender, here's the primary issue when they first open up: Will we still love them? We have to pass this test to earn the right to continue speaking into their lives. If we lead with judgment, we fail the test and our kids will be less likely to open up again. But there's more on the line here than our trust level with our children. If we fail this test, we've demonstrated that the love of God has limits and we've misrepresented the character of God to our children. On the flip side, if we pass this test and communicate that we love them always, we are also communicating the same is true of God.

Depending on the circumstances, it is often valuable to verbalize this truth. It can be very simple: "I want you to know something. God doesn't think any less of you because of this struggle you're having, and neither do I. We are both for you one hundred percent and will stay that way regardless of what happens." The path to these precious opportunities to demonstrate the heart of God starts with having regular, open-ended times of connection with your children. It's the best way to communicate that God knows them intimately and still wants to be around them.

Make no mistake, God is committed to demonstrating his love for them through your parenting. There is no better path to a child's heart than through the open door of a parent's love, and this love is demonstrated through the moments of transparency created in these anticipated conversations about everyday life. Slowly, our kids will learn that we are indeed interested in the fascinating and mundane parts of their lives, and they will open up more, including the difficult conversations. It's important to note that the everyday conversations hold equal importance with the difficult ones, though, because both show our tender care and concern for our kids. And that's what they need more than anything else—a safe space to connect and be real with us.

This will look different as our children grow older. Not only will the timing for these conversations become more convoluted due to social calendars and work schedules, but our kids will pull away from us and move closer to their peers as a natural part of their growth and development. In these seasons, we still want to create that safe space for them. It's even more important as they begin to explore the world and their place in it to have somewhere they know they are accepted, no matter what. It's the "no matter what" that's the key to this part of developing a mentally healthy family. We must protect the safety and sanctity of our family as a miniature community where nothing can sway our affection for our children. What a powerful way to give them roots to withstand the challenges life will bring their way.

ENGAGING WITH YOURSELF

1. Did your parents regularly and consistently engage with you about whatever was going on in your life? How did that make you feel?

2. How does it feel to know God knows everything about you? Does it stress you out, does it bring comfort, or do you just choose not to think about it much?

3. How does the idea that God is for us, period, influence your view of God? How can it influence your children's lives?

4. What's one of your biggest fears about becoming a safe space for your children to open up and talk about their life problems with you?

> ### Verse to Consider or Memorize
> *"What shall we say about such wonderful things as these? If God is for us, who can ever be against us?"*
> Romans 8:31

This is one of my favorite verses in the Bible because it speaks so clearly to God's stance toward us. No matter what, God is for us. Despite any poor decisions we have made, God is on our side. Even if we've made mistakes (who hasn't?), God is on our team. What a powerful concept for us to grasp and for us to teach our children. To the degree we can embody this truth in the core of our being, to that same degree we will walk in confidence. On the one hand, knowing that the creator God of the universe is on our team changes nothing, because we still have all the same struggles and all the same battles. But on the other hand, knowing that God is for us changes everything for just the reason that

Romans 8:31 promises—God is the greatest teammate we could imagine. Who has the power or authority to stand against God and, therefore, against us? Literally, nobody can. Let that sink in for a moment. Ponder that reality for a microsecond here. Nobody can stand against God and God is for you, for your children. This truth should cause your confidence to soar if you allow it to seep into your soul.

2

GOD IS PAYING ATTENTION TO US

"You know when I sit down or stand up.
You know my thoughts even when I'm far away."
Psalm 139:2

Engaging with the Bible

God Is Never Far Away

God is always paying attention to us, even in the little moments of our lives. This truth is trumpeted throughout the Bible, streaming from nearly every book in both the Old and New Testaments. Only, it doesn't often feel like this. We live our lives largely feeling distant or isolated from the God of the universe, if we're being honest. There are moments here and there when God seems to close the gap, but we mostly feel like we're on our own. Because of this fact, verses like Psalm 139:2 feel a bit like a bait and switch. It seems like God promises something and doesn't hold to it as we toil away on the earth, far away from God's presence, love, and guidance.

And what exactly does the verse mean when it says God knows my thoughts even when I'm far away anyway? I thought God was everywhere all at once, so how can we even be far away from God? That just doesn't make any sense. Let's consider this part of the passage a little closer and consider what it means because there's a powerful truth hidden within these words. Since God doesn't move away from us and is everywhere, then we must be the ones who move. And this is exactly the case—our activities move us away from the presence of God when we choose to live separate from him. We can develop habits and actions in which we act as though God isn't real, and this practical atheism builds a wall between us and God. We erect this wall with our choices, and we maintain this wall by continuing to live as though there were no God. Even in these situations, the Scriptures tell us that God knows our thoughts and so much more.

Our Hairs Are Numbered

Matthew 10:29–31 states, "What is the price of two sparrows—one copper coin? But not a single sparrow can fall to the ground without your Father knowing it. And the very hairs on your head are all numbered. So don't be afraid; you are more valuable to God than a whole flock of sparrows." Think about this for a moment: God knows the number of hairs on your head. This number constantly changes, doesn't it? Every time you brush your hair or comb your fingers through your hair, the number of hairs on your head changes. Or maybe you pull out some gray hair because of vanity. In all these situations, God keeps a running total of the hairs on your head. This demonstrates a deep, ongoing, intimate knowledge of who we are.

Now, there could be a couple of ways to think about this data-collecting aspect of God. On the one hand, we can think of God in the heavens, looking about a heavenly control room filled with gadgets and gauges showing the counts of various people's hairs and other odd little facts. This becomes nearly deistic, as though God were a disinterested observer of humanity who has little interest in involving himself in the affairs of men. This view of God might fit with our preconceptions of God, since we do often feel like we are set adrift at sea without a captain in life; but it's not very encouraging. And I don't think this is what Jesus was trying to communicate about God either.

Instead, another way to view this idea of God knowing intricate details of our lives is to stand in wonder at how deeply involved in our lives God must actually be. If God knows all the mundane and almost meaningless information about us and revels in it, how much more must God be engaged with the truly important aspects of our lives? Since we can trust that God knows shallow things about our lives like hair data, surely we can also trust God knows our deepest fears and deepest desires. Surely we can trust that God will never leave us. After all, why track the details of someone you don't care about at such an in-depth level? How could we imagine that God would just abandon us when he's already invested so much into knowing every aspect of us? And we know he won't because he has promised exactly that. The decisiveness of God's investment in our lives becomes vital when our mental health starts to waver. We might feel as though our mental health disqualifies us from God's interest in who we are and who we are becoming, but nothing could be further from the truth. No matter what thoughts occur in our heads, the value God places on our lives is unchanging.

Even when we choose to pull away from God by the way we live, God does not follow suit. God never withdraws from our lives, no matter how carefully we construct an existence without him. Our kids experience this same disconnect with God in their daily lives, and we can help them navigate these troubled spiritual waters. Before we can talk about the details of how to help our children, there's a bit of theology we need to cover together.

The Kingdom of God

The Bible is very clear that God is the Lord of the earth. The Scriptures are full of statements to this effect, calling him the God who owns the cattle on a thousand hills, the creator and upholder of the universe, and even the God who dwells outside of time. So it seems like God should be able to intervene at a moment's notice to right any wrongs that have happened on this planet. Yet this isn't the way God operates, because he believes wholeheartedly in the power of free will. God won't force his way into anyone's life, and God won't enforce his purposes when somebody doesn't want it. This is exactly where the problem began, many moons ago.

Adam and Eve were given authority over the garden of Eden and told to subdue the Earth and multiply upon it. They had no boundaries placed upon them, save one—do not eat of the Tree of the Knowledge of Good and Evil. God gave our first parents free will, a decision to make that would either hurt or help them. They chose poorly, and the repercussions of that decision have been echoing throughout the universe ever since. Satan took control of things on planet Earth. It's important to note he wasn't given control by God; he usurped the throne.

Since that moment, the world has been topsy-turvy because there is a false king on the throne of the world, bringing chaos and destruction with him. Romans chapter 8 says that even the Earth itself groans in anticipation of its redemption, the moment when God returns to the scene and sets everything right. But wait, didn't

God already fix everything in the life, ministry, death, burial, and resurrection of Jesus Christ? Yes and no. Jesus established that he was the rightful ruler of this universe, and his enthronement was confirmed by God in the resurrection.

The Already and the Not Yet

But he has yet to take his throne entirely. Even though Jesus is at the right hand of God, interceding on our behalf (Rom. 8:34), still the fullness of his authority on Earth remains unrealized. We live in what's commonly been called "the already and the not yet," a strange period that exists between the first and second comings of Jesus. In the first coming, Jesus demonstrated that he is the king of the universe; but it won't be until his second coming that we will see him established on his throne. In the meantime, we have glimpses of his glorious kingdom that shine through the dark and tumultuous times we now know. There are moments when we see clearly that the time is coming when every tear will be dried up, every wound will be healed, and even death will be banished from existence in the light of the goodness of God. In these spaces, we see the kingdom of God drawing near, on Earth as it is in heaven.

But there are also moments where we are left wondering why God hasn't shown up when we need him the most. God seems silent when we cry to him in prayer or distant when we are all alone. Just where is God, and why isn't he showing up? This is the "not yet" part of the kingdom of God. Satan has been told that the throne isn't his, and he has been defeated through the resurrection of Jesus, but he defiantly sits upon the throne anyway until the day he is forcibly removed . . . and that day has not come yet. So in the meantime, we are left with carnage and grace, disaster and redemption, sorrow and joy.

How the "Not Yet" Can Be Painful

The "not yet" of the kingdom causes pain in our lives and the lives of our children in three distinct ways: through our own bad choices, through the bad choices of others, and through direct intervention from the spiritual realm. Sometimes we can make bad choices that have direct negative impacts on our lives. It's important to note that these choices are not always what we would call sin; they are sometimes just bad choices. Maybe we choose to stay up until one a.m. reading a book when we have work in the morning. There's no sin in that choice, but it does have ramifications for the next day. There are far greater and more disastrous choices that are sinful and can bring destruction into our lives. Decisions like getting involved in drug abuse, pornography, infidelity, and theft in the workplace are all examples of sinful decisions that can affect our lives negatively. If the "already" were always here, we wouldn't have a sinful nature and we wouldn't have to worry about making bad decisions that bring chaos into our lives.

Sometimes we have nothing to do with the pain brought into our lives because we are victims of other people's actions. Here I think of my past as a survivor of child abuse. My dad was a drunk when I was growing up, and he was an angry drunk at that. He inflicted pain on me and my mom time after time, through no fault of our own. We were just the people who happened to be in front of him when he went off the deep end in a fit of rage. I think of my female friends who were sexually assaulted in their childhoods. They didn't do anything to earn or deserve this horrific thing. They were the victims of evil brought about by another person's choice. In an "already" world, these evils wouldn't exist, but we also live in a "not yet" world where the pain is real and it's not always our fault.

There are still other times when direct spiritual intervention is the root cause of pain. While not everyone will agree with me,

I believe people can become demon possessed or oppressed. I've seen it with my own eyes enough times to be convinced. These demons influence the decision-making power of individuals in such a dramatic way that it's hard to hold these people at fault for the decisions they've made; they need deliverance before they can be held accountable for their choices. This is a perilous and heart-rending journey for a person to take because the demons will fight against being cast out in sometimes dramatic ways. Freedom is possible, but pain remains until that freedom comes. As an example of this, Matthew 17 records the story of a boy who was demon-possessed and was often thrown into fire and water. While not all who are demonized are hurt in this way, there is always pain.

Regardless of whether the source of this "not yet" pain comes from our choices, someone else's choices, or direct spiritual intervention, we live in a world full of heartache. And this doesn't even touch on natural causes of pain like disease. Some people believe this too is ultimately the result of the poor choice in the garden of Eden, but I'm not fully sure where I personally land on that. Regardless, kingdom of God theology doesn't overlook or minimize this reality but rather tries to explain why an all-powerful and all-loving God doesn't do more to stop the terrible things that happen in this life. I look forward to the day when Jesus is rightfully enthroned as the king of this world and we no longer have to worry about "not yet" moments.

Daniel and Spiritual Intervention

Armed with this knowledge about the kingdom of God, we can understand better now how it can be so hard to survive in this world. It feels so lonely sometimes, and sometimes when we most need God or some touch from the divine, nothing can be found. An interesting event happens in Daniel 10 related to this idea of

God not being present in our hour of need. In this passage, Daniel was given a great vision of the future that he did not comprehend, and he became deeply disturbed by the vision. He decided to fast and pray until he was given understanding. After three weeks, an angel showed up to explain the vision to him.

I know, in a lot of ways this feels very different from our daily experiences. If we could get a vision and have an angel show up to explain it, all our problems would be gone, right? Hang tight with me; I promise I'm going somewhere good with this story. The angel tells Daniel that he had planned to come immediately and give Daniel an understanding of the vision, but a demonic prince kept him engaged in a battle for three weeks. Eventually, angelic reinforcements arrived, and the messenger was able to get away to talk to Daniel.

We must be careful about taking this story too far. It's not necessarily true that every time we don't hear from God, it's because of demonic interference. But, and this is important, sometimes that's exactly what's happening. Sometimes, the best thing we can do is keep holding on for dear life to what we know to be true from God while we wait for more clarity. In time, reinforcements will arrive, and we will get the insight, guidance, or support we've been waiting for. It just won't always arrive on our timeline.

Engaging Our Kids with This Truth

So now the question becomes how we engage our kids with these pretty heady concepts in a meaningful way. As you might imagine, it depends greatly upon the age of our kids, because we need to frame a conversation about the kingdom of God much differently with a teenager than with a four-year-old. At the same time, we need to be certain we aren't downplaying the natural-born spiritual capacity younger children can have; we should never assume something is too complex for our kids until we talk with them about it. Perhaps the greatest gifts children, especially younger children, bring to spiritual conversations are the ability to play, pray, and wonder without being weighed down by the complexities of life we have become all too familiar with.

Nevertheless, because of the disparity between how we need to interact on these topics, this section will be broken into age-group categories, with a series of ideas for each age range given to help bring awareness of God paying attention to us, the kingdom of God theology, and more related topics. Mental strength is developed in our kids at every age as they understand the remarkable truth that God is indeed paying attention to our every movement.

Ages Three to Seven

At these ages, we look to introduce spiritual concepts in ways that are engaging, interesting, and short. In other words, we need to hit quickly and get out. Before they know what's happened, our kids have had some spiritual truths embedded in their spirits, to be watered and carefully tended to over the years. We have the opportunity to communicate one big idea at a time with children this age because they simply don't have the attention span for more. Here are a couple of examples of how we could communicate with them concerning the big idea that God pays attention to us.

1. Read Matthew 10:30 to your kids. Ask them to count the number of hairs on their head or your head, and give them time to try to do it. Before frustration sets in, ask them how hard it is to try to do such a thing. Ask them how hard it would be to keep track of the hairs on their head every day, all the time. Remind them that God *always* knows the number of hairs on our heads. End the quick devotional time by telling them that God's love is

so deep that God knows *everything* about us, even the number of hairs on our heads.
2. Read Psalm 139:2 to your kids. Ask them to sit down, then stand up, then sit down, and then stand up again. Continue to have them do this, progressively moving faster and faster. If you do this well, then before you know it your kids will be giggling with delight at the sheer silliness of what you're doing, because it's nonsensical. Then remind them of what you just read, that God knows when we sit and when we stand. This means that every single time we stand up or sit down, God knows about it, even if we do it a hundred times in a row just to be silly. Ask them if they have any idea why God is keeping track of us when we sit down and stand up (they might not have any idea, and that's okay). Tell them it's because God loves us and wants to keep track of what's happening in our lives.

Ages Eight to Twelve

At these ages, children begin developmentally to be able to understand some intangible concepts, but only in small doses. Kids are very aware at this age of being treated too young and become sensitive to it, so it's important to treat them like their actual age. Many at this age start to become more serious as they shed the silliness of early childhood and appreciate being treated this way. The key for this time is to carefully tend the line between speaking over their heads and talking down to them as though they are five years old. Here is one way to meaningfully tend that line with this age range of kids:

Ask your kids if they can think of a time when God answered a prayer of theirs. If they don't have one, that's okay—you're going to coach them on how to keep track of prayers. Share a story of a time when God answered your prayers in a very specific way. Then tell them you will help them start a prayer journal. Present them with a fancy journal already labeled as a prayer journal. Ask them, "What is something you'd like to ask God for right now?" and tell them that nothing is too silly or too serious to ask God about. Pray with them for that thing, and then have them write that prayer in their prayer journal. Tell them to keep thinking and praying for that thing, and to write down in the journal when God answers their prayer. If your kids don't like writing, then you can modify this in a bunch of ways. Options include you writing the prayers down for them or having a bulletin board with unlined index cards for your kids to draw their prayer requests and pin them to the board.

Encourage them to open their prayer journal at least once a week to read about what they have been praying about and to remind themselves of the answers God has given them to their prayers. Teach them that listening to our prayers and answering them is one way God shows he pays attention to us. Coach your children that God won't always answer our prayers with a yes, but that God always listens and we can trust him with our deepest hurts.

Ages Thirteen to Eighteen

If you remember being an adolescent at all, you probably don't want to revisit it. All of us were our most awkward selves. Our hormones were running out of control, our bodies were changing, our emotions were out of whack, and everything was a hot mess. If that's where your kids are right now, start every thought about them with grace, because it's hard to be an adolescent. It's always been hard, but I believe it's harder today than it's ever been with the proliferation of social media, the way families continue to be broken, and the instability that surrounds teenagers. Note that kids this age become easily bored if we don't quickly prove that what we have to say matters to them, so we better prioritize relevance. At this age, we need to spend as much time talking with them as we do talking at them, so engaging in conversations instead of lectures is one key to keeping them interested. Here is one way to talk with adolescents about the idea of God paying attention to us:

Open your conversation with a time when you needed God to show up and he didn't, then talk about how that made you feel. Ask them if they've ever felt like God has abandoned them and how that felt for them. Read Psalm 139:2 and ask them what their response is to this verse—does it feel like a real promise or a bait and switch from God? Be willing to listen to whatever struggles they might throw out there in response to this question, without any judgment, frustration, or correction. The goal here is to give our adolescents a chance to open up about their lives, not to have correct theology.

Ask them if they'd be willing to try something new to see how faithful God is in their lives, something that you'd be doing alongside them and testing out to see if it works. Introduce the idea of a prayer journal in a similar way to what's described in the previous section, and commit to using a prayer journal alongside them to track God's movement in each other's lives. By admitting that you have space to grow in this as well, you're building camaraderie with your adolescent and inviting them to join you instead of speaking to them as an expert; this is invaluable and will do much to build rapport and trust with your child.

· ·

We've traveled a long road in this chapter. We've looked at the fact that God always pays attention to us. We've looked at the theology of the kingdom of God, and we've considered how Daniel's experience with his vision could be related to our own waiting periods with God. We've done a deep dive into how these ideas can be communicated to our kids at various ages. It's been a lot to cover, but let's end where we started—with the fact that God sees and adores us every day, all the time, period. God desperately loves us, never tires of us, and never has something better to do than to pay attention to us. Even when we are far from our best selves, God remains close to us.

ENGAGING WITH YOURSELF

1. How much do you personally struggle with the idea that God pays attention to all the details in your life because he seems absent from your life?

2. When you think about the three ways that the "not yet" of the kingdom of God can cause pain—poor personal choices, poor choices by others, or direct spiritual intervention—which do you think affects your life the most today?

3. What does the thought of starting a prayer journal for yourself stir in you? Do you think it would be challenging to encourage your children to start one?

4. What are your fears about engaging your children in spiritual conversations?

> ### Verse to Consider or Memorize
> *"If we had forgotten the name of our God
> or spread our hands in prayer to foreign gods,
> God would surely have known it,
> for he knows the secrets of every heart."*
>
> Psalm 44:20–21

God knows the secrets of every heart, even when we long to wander away from God's best for us. God understands the inclinations of our hearts and always pays attention, even though he might not always be intervening the way we'd like. Let us not forget the nature of our God, for his goodness truly is from everlasting to everlasting. Instead, let's choose to remember the ways God is faithful through practices like journaling and rehearsing the victories God has accomplished for us with our children. Let's build faith in our hard seasons and our good seasons alike by remembering the ways of God.

3

GOD SEES US

*"You see me when I travel
and when I rest at home.
You know everything I do."*

Psalm 139:3

Engaging with the Bible

What Does It Mean to Be Seen?
This might feel similar to what we covered in Chapter One, because we talked about God knowing everything about us and still loving us. It might also seem to be the same as Chapter Two, since we talked about God knowing us when we are near or far. But there's something unique about this verse, something that hits differently, and it's all because of that opening phrase: *You see me*. Being seen is a powerful thing, especially in a world that minimizes us and makes us feel invisible or unimportant. In this belittling world, God stands against all that and defiantly says, "I see you." It's simple but profound.

We are seen and understood by the creator of the universe. Think about what being seen means in the context of other relationships. Imagine yourself in a fight with a friend, and it's a fight because they aren't listening to what you're saying. Instead, you keep talking past each other without paying attention to the heart behind the words being spoken. Until, finally, something breaks in the conversation (if we can even call an argument a conversation), and you say something like this: "Now you understand what I'm saying. It took long enough, but you get me." This is what it means to be seen. It's more than a physical or mental awareness of someone's presence. It's a validation of their entire being. Sometimes we exchange the words "being heard" for "being seen" in this context because they essentially mean the same thing. There is a nuance of being understood, of being counted as worthwhile, and even of having an opinion worth listening to. During moments of mental health struggle, we will often feel like nobody, including God, understands or sees us. We feel completely isolated, misunderstood, and uncared for. Yet we can know because of this verse that God sees and implicitly understands what we are going through.

In this verse, the psalmist declares that God always sees him. God always validates David. God recognizes his inherent worth regardless of what he might be doing at the moment. Always, God looks at David (and at us) and sees someone worth paying attention to. This understanding of God's view of us brings peace, especially in moments when we feel invisible. But a frustration can also rise in moments of crisis. If God sees me, if God recognizes the validity of my existence, and if God understands what I am going through, then why isn't he acting? Sometimes we want more from God than to be aware of us when we are struggling. We want God to intervene on our behalf, and it hurts when he doesn't. Kingdom of God theology like we talked about in the last chapter can somewhat limit the pain, but we are still left with this nagging question: Where is God when we need him most? This is a question our children will be struggling through as well when tough times hit them, especially because they're still developing physically, psychologically, and hormonally. In other words, everything is harder for our kids than it is for us.

Hagar and the God Who Sees

We can find comfort in times of trials in the story of Hagar (see Gen. 16). Hagar was Sarai's servant, and she was put in a very uncomfortable position. After Sarai realized she was barren, she gave Hagar to her husband, Abram, to sleep with him. Hagar became pregnant, and then things got dicey for everyone. Hagar began to treat Sarai with contempt, so Sarai complained to Abram and told him to deal with her. Abram put the responsibility back on Sarai, and she treated Hagar poorly enough that Hagar left the camp. Keep a few things in mind here. First, it's not like Abram and Sarai lived in a city, where Hagar could just rent an apartment for herself and her unborn child. No, they lived in the middle of nowhere, so Hagar ran away blindly with no idea of where she might end up. Second, Hagar was Sarai's servant, and she lived in a time when women had very few rights. She couldn't go find a job for herself to provide for her fledgling family. Lastly, even if she had somehow found a way to meet her needs, she would have been looked down upon because of her unwed pregnancy. So we see severe desperation in Hagar's actions. She needed direction and hope and intervention from someone.

And that's when God showed up. The angel of the Lord found Hagar by a spring of water along the road. He asked her where she came from and where she was going. Markedly, Hagar only said she was running from her mistress and ignored the second question, most likely because she didn't have a plan or know where she was going. She needed to get away from Sarai, and that's all she knew. The angel told her to return to Sarai, that he would give her a son, and to call him *Ishmael*, which means "God hears." The angel went on to speak of Ishmael's destiny and future. Hagar then called God *El Roi*, which means "the God who sees me." Here's an amazing fact about this moment. Hagar is the first person to give a name to God. Hagar is a slave woman; she's not a part of God's promised line; and she's on the run from the very person God chose to make his covenants with. In her society, she was a nobody. It's a surprise that we even hear her story in the biblical narrative or know her name because she's not a part of the promise from God. Yet the angel of the Lord finds her in the wilderness, soothes her broken spirit, and gives her direction and hope.

God can do the same for us when we run for legitimate reasons from our very real problems and find ourselves bereft of hope. God can find us by the side of the road in the middle of nowhere and instill purpose and destiny in our lives. God can give us the privilege of calling him a special name that is known only to us because of the unique way he's shown up in our lives. It doesn't matter if we are important enough in the eyes of the world for God to invest in us, because God sees us. But what do we do if he doesn't? How are we supposed to respond if God doesn't find us and give us hope and an intimate view of our best possible future? To answer this question, we turn to another passage of Scripture.

Contemplating the Love of God
We won't always have an "El Roi" moment where an angel of the Lord gives us the courage to move forward. Sometimes, we are left to our own devices because we live in a busted world. In those moments, we still can make choices that encourage our faith and tenacity or tear us down. These moments might be the most important ones in our lives, as they form the basis for whether we will be able to withstand the tornadoes that life inevitably brings

our way. There is a profound passage in the book of Ephesians that can guide us through these challenging times and show us the way forward. Ephesians 3:17–20 says,

> Christ will make his home in your hearts as you trust in him. Your roots will grow down into God's love and keep you strong. And may you have the power to understand, as all God's people should, how wide, how long, how high, and how deep his love is. May you experience the love of Christ, though it is too great to understand fully. Then you will be made complete with all the fullness of life and power that comes from God. Now all glory to God, who is able, through his mighty power at work within us, to accomplish infinitely more than we might ask or think.

There is a lot to unpack in these few verses that apply to those moments when it doesn't seem like God is going to show up, even though we need exactly that to happen. The first sentence teaches us that Christ makes his home in our hearts *as we trust* in him. It's a give-and-take nature here, where Jesus, through the Holy Spirit, becomes more and more obvious in our lives as our trust in him grows. Stated differently, the biggest barrier to the presence of God in our lives becomes unbelief. This is a hard word, but it's even supported in the Gospels. Jesus found himself unable to perform many miracles in his hometown when he visited because of their unbelief. Unbelief creates a spiritual blockage and prevents God from doing mighty things in our lives.

Now, it's very important to say that unbelief or lack of faith isn't the only variable, because far too many people have been left wounded on the road of life by this lie. No, I'm not saying that God isn't working miracles in your life because you lack faith. Instead,

I am pointing out the inescapable reality that faith ebbs and flows, and this can create hindrances or open pathways for God to move. If you find yourself in a space seemingly bereft of God's presence, one question to ask is whether you have erected a barrier of unbelief in your life. Again, it's not the only path forward, but it can be an important stepping stone to unleash the presence of God.

The next concept that pops out of this passage is that we can grow roots in God's love. This is precisely what I've been talking about with tenacity. The core path to being tenacious is being connected to the source of God's love in our lives. The promise is that these roots will keep us strong, and strength is important when difficult times come, because we will get weary. This love is not only something supernatural that can't be understood though. The third element to grasp in this passage is that we can understand the width, length, height, and depth of God's love. This means we can, on some level, intellectually appreciate the grandeur of God's love for us.

How can we do this though? There are myriad ways, but here are two: remember the times God has come through for us personally and remember the stories in Scripture when God showed up in powerful ways. If we can bring to mind those precious moments when God showed himself real to us, then we will be able to strengthen ourselves in the Lord when it seems like he is absent, because we will see his character personally and intimately. Second, if we read the events told about in Scripture as real things that happened to real people, not as mythical fables, then we will see how God intervenes in the lives of those he loves. This will help us to grasp the enormity of God's love, which will shore us up against the doubts that will inevitably come when things aren't going the way we want them to go.

Once we remind ourselves of the grand love of God, the promise of this passage becomes that we will be made complete with life and power from God. I confess I don't know exactly what this means, but it fills me with excitement at the prospect of finding out. This fourth component of Ephesians 3 fills me with hope. I would love to walk in the fullness of life and power promised here. I imagine it means doubt will be silenced in our lives, the love of God will pierce any challenge life throws at us and render it inert, and we will walk in an awareness of the presence of God that we don't currently possess. This sounds like one tremendous promise, almost beyond imagining from where I currently sit. I believe that's why Paul followed this promise up with a declaration of God's mighty power. God can accomplish more than we can even imagine because he is grander than our thoughts can fathom. This is why Isaiah 55:9 can say, "For just as the heavens are higher than the earth, so my ways are higher than your ways and my thoughts higher than your thoughts." We aren't talking about a God like the Greek gods, who were just bigger and more powerful human beings, subject to all the whims and sins of humanity. No, we are talking about a being completely different from us in every way, who is able to accomplish the impossible, and who delights in doing just that.

So we can turn to Ephesians 3 and Isaiah 55 when times get rough, and we can point our children to these same verses. We can decide to trust in the sureness of God's love as demonstrated to us in Jesus Christ, even when it feels like everything is falling apart. We can look to our past and the pasts of others who've followed our God and encourage ourselves that God is still faithful.

Engaging Our Kids with This Truth

We simply must find the time and space to engage our children with this idea. It is one of the most meaningful components of a mentally strong faith, one that can withstand the arduous challenges of this life. Our kids must know that God sees them, validates them, accepts them, and sees value in their being. Without this context, the challenges of life may very well pull them away from faithfulness to God because they never had the chance to develop tenacity.

Ages Three to Seven
While we might imagine that this is too complex a topic for youngsters to grasp, we can definitely build a foundation for them to understand being seen by God. Here are a couple of quick ideas to try out with your young ones to begin establishing this idea in their minds and hearts:

1. Play a few rounds of hide and seek with your kids, making sure to tell them they need to find the absolute best place ever to hide every time. Make a big deal out of not being able to find them, no matter how obvious the hiding spot is. After two to three rounds, ask them this: "Did you know that God always sees where you are, no matter where you might be hiding? That's pretty cool, isn't it?"
2. Ask your kids to tell you about the last time they were scared or angry or felt all alone. Respond by telling them about a time that you felt the same, keeping the story at less than a minute if possible. Ask them how they know, or if they do know, that God sees them right now. Then remind them that God sees us and cares about us, even when we're afraid or alone.

Ages Eight to Twelve
Read Psalm 139:3 and tell your children that God always sees us, no matter where we go or what we are doing. In two to three minutes, tell them a story about when God showed up in an "El Roi"

kind of way in your life. If you can't think of one, retell the story of Hagar or read it from the Bible. Remind your kids that God always looks down from heaven, paying attention to the things that happen in our lives.

Ask your kids to say out loud the biggest number they can think of, and then tell them to imagine a building that many feet tall. Read Ephesians 3:18 and tell them that God's love is taller than even that building.

Ages Thirteen to Eighteen
Read the story of Hagar with your children and ask them to put themselves in Hagar's shoes at various points in the story. Ask them to imagine being pregnant with someone else's kid and being abused by their master, and it getting so bad that they ran away into the wilderness. What thought might have been going through Hagar's head when she ran? Ask them to wrestle with the idea that God sent Hagar back to Sarai even though she was being abused—what does this say about God, and why might he have done that? You don't have to have answers to these questions, by the way. We're just trying to get our kids to engage with the stories in Scripture as though they actually happened, because they did.

Ask your children if they've ever been as desperate as Hagar probably was on the side of the road, and what they did at that moment. Did they ask God for help, try to figure it out on their own, or turn to their friends? No judgment here, just again looking to engage them in conversation.

Lead your children in a simple prayer like this: God, give me eyes to see you in my life. Teach me how to slow down and find you when I'm in desperate times and when things are going well. I want to know that I am seen by you like you saw Hagar.

ENGAGING WITH YOURSELF

1. How difficult is it for you to believe that you are seen by God the way Hagar was seen by God?

2. Why do you think God sent Hagar back to Sarai even though she was being abused by Sarai? (There's no right answer to this question because the Bible is silent on this issue.)

3. How regularly do you consider the depth and breadth and width and height of God's love for you? Is it more of an afterthought in your life, or is it something you regularly consider?

4. Why do you think understanding God's love can allow us to grow roots in the tree of our life?

Verse to Consider or Memorize

"Now all glory to God, who is able, through his mighty power at work within us, to accomplish infinitely more than we might ask or think."

Ephesians 3:20

It's far too easy to think of God as small and incapable of intervening in our lives. Maybe we even convince ourselves that our lives or our kids' lives are such a mess because he isn't able. Or we might lack the imagination to see how God could intervene in our lives. Sometimes this happens because we are so encumbered by the situation that we can't see a way out of it. Nothing could be further from the truth though. This God we serve can accomplish grander things than we can even put our minds to. God can do things that astound us. The Bible is full of amazing moments like this, but sometimes we simply don't take the Bible or the stories of other people seriously enough to think they are real stories. We relegate them to myths. Let's instead allow faith to rise in our spirits as we consider the grandeur of God so that we can engage from a place of faith and expectation. Repeatedly in the New Testament, we see that faith moved Jesus and the apostles to act, so let's be among the crowds that believe instead of doubting. Who knows what will happen as a result?

4

GOD KNOWS OUR WORDS

"You know what I am going to say even before I say it, Lord."
Psalm 139:4

Engaging with the Bible

Words Demonstrate the Heart

We've all been there before. In the heat of the moment, some words pop out of our mouths before we think through them, how they'll be received, and what they mean. The damage is done—and once words escape our mouths, there can be no takebacks. We can't undo the pain we've caused because it's too late. Sadly, the place this happens most for many people is with their children. For some reason, we equate the safety and generosity of the home with people who will tolerate our negative and ill-spoken words, so we guard our tongues less with our families than with others. As a result, we end up wounding our families more than almost anyone else, because they aren't going anywhere. This is terrible, but there's a modicum of truth to it. If we sass our boss, we might get fired. If we smack down our friends, they might distance themselves from us. But where exactly will our kids go? They're stuck with us, so we let our tongues fly.

Sometimes it looks different from this too. There are times when we stay completely unaware that our words have caused wounds, or maybe we recognize that our family is shrinking back from us but we don't know what has happened. Especially with our kids, we must take the initiative to find out what's happened and try to resolve it. It doesn't matter if we intended to hurt anyone—what matters is that we caused pain. We simply must keep short accounts, particularly with our family. When I say "keep short accounts," what I mean is to not let frustrations or agitation or anything stay unspoken between us and our families. Ephesians 4:26 says we should not let the sun go down on our anger. It's not always possible to deal with our emotions that quickly, but we should still strive to guard our hearts against bitterness.

The Bible has a lot to say about guarding our lips, but let's start with Psalm 139:4. God knows what we will say before we even say it. God is never surprised when we lose our cool. Never even once has God been shocked by the words that erupt out of us, no matter how foul those words might be. God is aware of the weapons we wield with our words because he knows our hearts. Jesus gives us a very important concept about words and where they come from in Luke 6:43–45 when he says:

> A good tree can't produce bad fruit, and a bad tree can't produce good fruit. A tree is identified by its fruit. Figs are never gathered from thornbushes, and grapes are not picked from bramble bushes. A good person produces good things from the treasury of a good

heart, and an evil person produces evil things from the treasury of an evil heart. What you say flows from what is in your heart.

. . . .

Often people will say something like what Jesus ends with by stating that our hearts were made clear from our words, and there is certainly truth in this, but there is also more to uncover on this topic. Jesus isn't just saying that our words reflect what is in our hearts. He says it's impossible for a so-called evil person to produce good fruit, because they are evil; and it's equally impossible for a so-called good person to produce evil fruit, because they are good. If you're anything like me, you recognize that all of us are a mixture of good and bad things, so it's easy to disregard this idea that Jesus is proposing. It seems unreasonable to categorize people into "good" and "evil" piles—who would even make that decision in the first place? The key concept in Jesus's words is the idea of a treasury, and this sheds light on what he means in the first place. A treasury isn't a single piece of gold or silver but a vast collection of items. The US Treasury doesn't just have one twenty-dollar bill in it. No, it's stuffed to the gills with cash.

So it is with our hearts. We are stuffed to the gills with something. Again, no one is fully good or evil, so it's never going to be as simple as Jesus seems to imply in this one story. Jesus does leave some nuance in his story, because we can still pull rotten or sour grapes off the vine, but I digress. Now we circle back to the fruit, the words that come out of someone's mouth. If it seems like we have a treasure trove of anger or a vast amount of bitterness based on our words, then this tells us something about the contents of our hearts. And this is a touchpoint for us as parents, a place for us to engage with our kids about the words coming out of their mouths. If it seems like nothing but snark comes out of them, then this indicates a deeper problem.

We have to resist the urge to deal only with the issue at hand and choose instead to dig deeper. We must learn to ask the harder questions that sit beneath the surface of the current agitation and engage with what's really going on. Yes, we need to deal with the pain caused by the words that were said, and we'll get to how to do that well later in this chapter, but let's not miss this opportunity to engage our kids with more meaningful conversations. This is the stuff of parenting, after all, diving deep into our kids' hearts to help them understand themselves better. Let's not forget that our kids are still developing, so they oftentimes can't explain what's going on. They need a guide to help them figure everything out, and we are that guide.

There are times when the treasury of our heart yields more confusion than anything else. This is particularly true during a "down season" with our mental health. Perhaps our depression is skewing our experiences in life, so we feel as though the world is aligned against us. This might cause us to lash out in bitterness because we perceive that we're all alone in the world. Our anxiety might tell us that everything coming against us is just too much to handle, and we might allow irritation to taint our words as a result. In either case, we have work to do. We must figure out why the treasury of our heart is filled with nastiness, purge that nastiness, and get back to giving life with our words.

Our Tongues Are a Fire

The Bible doesn't mince words when it comes to the power of the tongue. Proverbs 18:21 says, "The tongue can bring death or life." You've probably felt both life and death from the words that have come out of others' mouths. Words of affirmation from important people in our lives can be like a breeze on a warm summer night. They can refresh our souls and restore hope and dignity to our spirits. Words spoken in anger or out of strife can bring frustration, agitation, and discouragement.

We can never underestimate the power of words spoken to our kids. James 3:6–8 adds a sobering warning: "Among all the parts of the body, the tongue is a flame of fire. It is a whole world of wickedness, corrupting your entire body. It can set your whole life on fire, for it is set on fire by hell itself. People can tame all kinds of animals, birds, reptiles, and fish, but no one can tame the tongue. It is restless and evil, full of deadly poison." With words like this found in the Bible, it might seem as though it's hopeless for any of us to control our tongues. Goodness, set on fire by hell and corrupting your entire body? How are we to have any hope of making wise choices in this context?

The contrast between Proverbs 18 and James 3 must be understood here. It's not just death that comes from words. It's not only hellfire that emanates from our tongue. Life and hope can be the end result of our words too. But this brings up the question, how can we reconcile these two concepts in a meaningful way? We must recognize that all of us will have at least moments where our tongues betray what dwells in our hearts. We will all make mistakes with the words that come out of our mouths. There's no avoiding this because we are all fallen and imperfect people. Even the kindest among us will slip up once in a while. The question isn't just how we can normalize kinder words but also what we do after we've made a mistake with our mouths.

Repentance Is the Key
Since we will all make regrettable decisions with our words, we have to know what to do after those moments, both as a model for our children and for our own spiritual well-being. Often, we think an apology is sufficient. We say hurtful things to someone, and then we say "I'm sorry" and think everything should suddenly

get better. That's just not true though. It never has been and it never will be. An apology doesn't require a response from the other person in any way, and indeed, the only response we expect after an apology is something like "It's okay." The biblical response to any sin, including a sin of words, is repentance, but this is a difficult concept to understand well. Guidance on the distinct components of repentance can be found in Jeremiah 31:18–19: "I have heard Israel saying, 'You disciplined me severely, like a calf that needs training for the yoke. Turn me again to you and restore me, for you alone are the Lord my God. I turned away from God, but then I was sorry. I kicked myself for my stupidity! I was thoroughly ashamed of all I did in my younger days.'"

The first element of repentance is a change of mind. We can see in the Jeremiah passage that Israel had turned away from God and then recognized the error of her ways. She cried out to God to change her ways because she longed to draw close to God again. This brings us to the next element of repentance: a change of direction. It's not enough to simply acknowledge the error of our ways and do nothing different. No, we have to also change the way we act. Lastly, there must be some sense of sorrow or sadness about the sins we have committed. In Jeremiah, Israel says she was ashamed of her actions from when she was younger. This is particularly instructive for us. While there is no condemnation for those in Christ, it's not unreasonable to feel sorrow or sadness over our mistakes. Indeed, it's necessary for us to truly be able to repent, because otherwise, we just go through the motions.

Let's put this all together into a conversational package around repentance so there's a clear picture of what it looks like to repent when our tongues have caused us to sin. Here's an example of what repentance would verbally look like with our children (or someone else even): "I realize that the words I used were painful to you. You deserve better than this, and I recognize that now.

I made a mistake, one I regret. Would you please forgive me?" That's a lot different than an "I'm sorry" for several reasons. We're taking responsibility for our poor actions, we're recognizing that the person we sinned against deserved better than we gave them, and we're asking for forgiveness. The request for forgiveness is the most important part of this repentance package. We give the person we sinned against a chance to accept us back into their graces or not. An "I'm sorry" doesn't give this choice because it's often not as sincere as repentance but is more akin to a perfunctory social cue.

This brings up an interesting question of how quickly we should try to make things right with those we've hurt. We should seek relational restoration as soon as possible, but the Bible has more to say on this topic. In the Sermon on the Mount in Matthew 5:22–24, Jesus says,

> But I say, if you are even angry with someone, you are subject to judgment! If you call someone an idiot, you are in danger of being brought before the court. And if you curse someone, you are in danger of the fires of hell.
>
> So if you are presenting a sacrifice at the altar in the Temple and you suddenly remember that someone has something against you, leave your sacrifice there at the altar. Go and be reconciled to that person. Then come and offer your sacrifice to God.

Again we are faced with the reality that our words can truly harm others, but Jesus highlights that they endanger us as well. He counsels us to pause our rituals of worship as soon as we realize there is unfinished business with someone else. This is startling because we think God always wants our worship, but Jesus says otherwise. Think about that for a moment. Consider how different our world would be if we kept short accounts with everyone. Here's how that might look practically: Every Saturday afternoon, you could spend a bit of time cycling through your week, thinking about whether you've offended anyone with your words. If you have, repent and seek forgiveness. As Jesus said, be reconciled to that person before you go to worship your God.

Engaging Our Kids with This Truth

While this is going to look different for your seven-year-old than your teenager, there are some common elements we can address now. The first and best question to ask when you notice a pattern of unhealthy words coming from one of your kids is "What's going on in your heart right now?" This surprising question often catches your kid off guard. They might blow you off and continue with their attack, and it's okay if that's what happens. If you're blown off in the moment, then make a conscious decision to bring it up again when heads have cooled. This conversation would start with a statement like this: "I've noticed that you've had a bit of a short fuse lately. Is there some thought or something happening in your life that's making you respond in this way? It's not like you, and I'm worried."

If they stop and engage you in the conversation at any point, congratulations—you've captured your kid's heart in a precious moment. Don't waste it. Listen to whatever they say and affirm it, even if you think they're dead wrong. This isn't the time to correct any misconceptions they might have about you or life. No, this is the time for listening and agreeing. You may need to qualify your agreement with a statement like, "I can see how you might feel that way." But it's vital you validate them at this moment and stand by them. Part of mental strength is recognizing that we don't always have everything together in this life, and we need to model this reality to our children. As we gain a more accurate view of ourselves, and as our kids do the same, together we can grow deeper roots in Christ to withstand life's challenges. Now let's dive into how each age group might respond to this conversation and how you can model repentance to them.

Ages Three to Seven
Your youngster may not be able to describe why they're feeling sad or angry or lonely inside. Indeed, it might be that all they can verbalize is the feeling they have, so it's important to not push them too hard for details. We can't always ask this age group why they're feeling a certain emotion because they simply haven't developed enough physiologically and mentally to know how to examine themselves and answer this question. It will put a burden on them that they can't manage, and it will cause frustration for you. Instead, make it seem like you're switching topics by asking about their day at school or wherever else they were. Find out if something stirred up disappointment or agitation in them by asking for details about their day. Ask if they enjoyed certain parts of their day better than others, or if there was a part of the day that didn't go well for them. In this way, you will be able to hopefully identify the root cause of why they had an explosion of negative energy toward you. Keep in mind that, especially at this age, sometimes they're just tired or hungry or both. Let's be honest here—it's the same with all of us. Sometimes we just need a snack or a nap to be able to recover a decent perspective on the day.

There will be moments when we need to seek forgiveness from our young ones because of our own harsh words. The best way to do this is to keep it short and simple. The wording could be something like this: "I love you, but I didn't treat you like I love you when I spoke those mean words to you. Can you forgive me?" You might need to talk with them about what forgiveness means. The easiest explanation for forgiveness in this context is this: forgiveness means you don't think about the mean things I said anymore when you think about me. It's vital at this age to keep short accounts because, otherwise, we can stunt the emotional and social growth of our children. If they start to believe they're less than because of our words, the harm can be monumental and long-term, so we want to avoid this at all costs.

Ages Eight to Twelve
In contrast with younger children, we can reasonably expect that a child in this age range will have a better understanding about what has caused them to be "off" for the day. They might be able to tell you that their friend said something mean to them or one of their teachers gave them a bad grade. They might even be able to tell you how it made them feel when this happened. They also might not be able to do this, so don't press too hard if they start to freeze; that might only make things worse. The key thing to understand about this age group is that they aren't able to compartmentalize, at all. A bad day at school obviously and immediately equates to a bad day at home for the simple reason that they're the same person experiencing both scenarios. It's important to remember that compartmentalizing doesn't happen often at this age, because we might otherwise put unrealistic expectations on our children. Instead of asking them to treat us differently because we aren't the people who wounded them or upset them, we should step forward in love and comfort. They might reject our advances, but they will still remember our kindness later and appreciate our attempts.

If we need to be reconciled with one of our children in this age group, the most important thing to remember is that they need space to process emotions. While a preschooler might immediately forgive us, a child this age might need to sit with their pain for a while before they are comfortable forgiving us. We need to allow this space to exist and gently encourage them to move toward forgiveness. We can even speak to them about how simmering frustration can turn into bitterness, but we have to do this carefully and with gentleness, or it will seem as though we're trying to coerce them toward a forgiveness they aren't ready to give.

Ages Thirteen to Eighteen

As we've discussed in prior chapters, adolescents have a lot going on in their lives, and most of it is confusing. It's not very realistic to expect a point A to point B conversation about their attitudes to happen, because any number of events or emotions or hormones could be influencing the way they're acting on a given day. Indeed, trying to nail this down could very well lead to additional regrettable words between the two of you. Instead of trying to address sources for poor word choices with adolescents, the best way to approach them is to let them know unequivocally that you're their advocate and their biggest fan, even when they're not being kind. Grace becomes the byword for this season, and if you're wondering why, try to remember what it's like being a teen and then make it ten times more stressful (because it's more stressful today than when you were growing up, I promise).

When we make a mistake with our words, our adolescent will let us know, either by sassing us back or by shutting down and pulling away from us. Neither is healthy, so in an ideal world, we'd avoid this altogether. Alas, we live in a world where tongues are set on fire from hell sometimes and we sometimes speak out of the treasuries of evil that we have in our hearts, so damage will unfortunately happen. We have to address this head-on and not shy away from owning our mistakes and repenting from them. The most important thing here is to not be repeat offenders, because adolescents can spot a fake from miles away. We better make sure we mean it when we ask for forgiveness, and we need to do everything in our power to not repeat the same mistake over and over again. This stirs mistrust in our adolescents and makes them more prone to say they won't forgive us, which again sets the stage for bitterness. And that bitterness would in part lay at our feet for giving our kids a reason to disbelieve us.

ENGAGING WITH YOURSELF

1. How often do you find yourself having a short fuse with your children, and why do you think that might be the case?

2. How difficult is it for you to move beyond "I'm sorry" and into repentance and seeking forgiveness? What was modeled to you as a child?

3. When you think about how the Bible presents the tongue, do you think it's unfair or reasonable in its portrayal of the good and evil that is possible through our words?

4. How else do you think you can engage your kids to know the reasons behind their frustrations and agitations?

> **Verse to Consider or Memorize**
>
> *"Now repent of your sins and turn to God, so that your sins may be wiped away. Then times of refreshment will come from the presence of the Lord."*
>
> Acts 3:19–20

This beautiful promise from God comes through the mouth of Peter. If we repent of our sins, they will be washed away; but there's more. Not only will we have freedom from our sins, a powerful thing, but we will also have times of refreshment from God. When our words put us in a world of hurt because of estranged relationships, one thing we need is the presence of the Lord. God brings peace and a welcoming spirit like nothing else.

5

GOD IS ALL AROUND AND WITHIN US

*"You go before me and follow me.
You place your hand of blessing on my head."*
Psalm 139:5

Engaging with the Bible

God Goes before Us

It might feel like we're left alone in this world to fend for ourselves, but the Bible is full of promises that say otherwise. It's vital for us to grab hold of these promises for ourselves and to help our children grab hold of the same promises. One specific example of God's promise of presence is that he will go before us. God prepares the way for us to walk into different circumstances. An obvious example of when God did this was with the people of Israel when they escaped slavery in Egypt. They always had a physical manifestation of God's presence with them, a pillar of clouds during the day and a pillar of fire during the night. In this way, Israel knew when and where to travel because God was leading them. One fascinating moment related to the pillar of the presence of God is found in Exodus 14:19. Israel was being pursued by Egypt's army and in danger of being overtaken. This is where we pick up the story. "Then the angel of God, who had been leading the people of Israel, moved to the rear of the camp. The pillar of cloud also moved from the front and stood behind them."

We can learn a lot from this moment in Israel's history. God moved the pillar to the back of the people of Israel to provide them with protection from harm. God will sometimes do the same with us, even though the details will be different. By his presence, God will keep us safe from harm that's going to befall us. While the Israelites were quite aware of what God was doing, we might not always be in the same situation. On the contrary, we may have no idea at the moment that God is keeping us safe. We might only find out later, or we might never find out. Either way, God's actions keep us safe as he did for the Israelites by moving the pillar of clouds between Egypt and Israel.

God proves over and over again to be the one who smooths our paths. We see this characteristic of God shown in the promise given to Joshua by Moses in Deuteronomy 31:8— "Do not be afraid or discouraged, for the Lord will personally go ahead of you. He will be with you; he will neither fail you nor abandon you." I love the inclusion of the word "personally" in this promise. God is not sending someone on his behalf, perhaps a powerful angel or cherubim to help Joshua. No, God will personally show up and demonstrate power through the military victories Joshua will have. This is related to the promises Joshua receives later when he's told that wherever he puts his foot, he will have victory, and nobody will be able to stand against him. The reason Joshua became so mighty in battle is that God went before him and went with him into battle.

We're privileged to have these same types of promises given to us through Jesus. Though none of us is likely to wage war to create a new country, God promises to be with us. Jesus promises that he will not leave us as orphans in this world in John 14:18. The author of Hebrews assures us that Jesus is the same yesterday, today, and forever, and this is important in light of how the book of Hebrews opens in 1:1–3:

> Long ago God spoke many times and in many ways to our ancestors through the prophets. And now in these final days, he has spoken to us through his Son. God promised everything to the Son as an inheritance, and through the Son he created the universe. The Son radiates God's own glory and expresses the very character of God, and he sustains everything by the mighty power of his command.

In other words, God said everything he had to say in the person of Jesus. Jesus reflects perfectly the identity and character of God. This means that just like Jesus is the same throughout all time, so God remains unchanging too. We can look at how God went before the nation of Israel to preserve and protect them and claim that characteristic for ourselves. We must be careful not to take on the promises of Israel directly, because these are promises given at a specific time for a specific nation under a different covenant, but still, we can cling to the truth that God goes before those he loves.

God Is behind Us

The psalmist declares that God not only is before us but also goes behind us. What exactly does this mean, and how does it apply to our parenting? It doesn't mean that God cleans up our messes like a toddler's parent. No, more often than not we are held to the consequences of our decisions. Rather, it means that God washes over situations with grace. Second Corinthians 2:15 says, "Our lives are a Christ-like fragrance rising up to God." But there will be times when the smell we leave behind in our interactions with others isn't exactly the fragrance of Christ. Instead, it might be the lingering odor of being rushed, rude, or uncaring. In these situations, God can come behind and leave his fragrance instead of what we've left of our own accord.

This has direct application to our parenting and our children because sometimes our "stinkiest" moments happen with our kids. We lose track of time or lose patience with them and before we know it, we blow up at them over something inconsequential. Even when we ask for forgiveness as we talked about in the previous chapter, there is an opportunity for hurt to remain. Yet God in loving-kindness often washes those wounds away and replaces them with love.

God Is upon and within Us

David says God is upon us, and the New Testament adds that God is within us through the Holy Spirit that seals our salvation. Here's a powerful promise about the Holy Spirit that's easily missed because of the translations or definitions of the words used. Ephesians 1:13–14 (NIV) says, "You also were included in Christ when you heard the message of truth, the gospel of your salvation. When you believed, you were marked in him with a seal, the promised Holy Spirit, who is a deposit guaranteeing our inheritance until the redemption of those who are God's possession—to the praise of his glory." This word *deposit* is a Greek word meaning "earnest," which is how the King James Version translates the word. An earnest is a nonrefundable deposit, meaning that if a person walks away from a transaction, they lose whatever money or property they put down as a deposit.

Think about this for a moment—God is so committed to us that he gave the Holy Spirit as a nonrefundable deposit of our future inheritance. If God walks away from us, then he also walks away from the Holy Spirit. God would rather break up the Trinity than walk away from us. This is a powerful truth when we're on the back end of a horrific mistake, perhaps one that costs us financially or relationally. We might be telling ourselves lies, things like, "You're worthless" or "Nobody could ever trust or love you." Into this vortex of mental chaos, God speaks and says, "I am with you." In other words, this intimacy offered to us through the Holy Spirit isn't going anywhere. The reason is powerful when we sometimes believe God gets fed up with us, regrets drawing near to us, and maybe even wants to renegotiate his contract for us, so to speak. But the down payment of the Holy Spirit demonstrates unequivocally that God is "all in" on us.

The benefits of having the Holy Spirit within us are hard to quantify, but it's an important element to begin to understand, if only for the sake of dialoguing with our kids about what it means. Here is a summary of some of the many things the Holy Spirit accomplishes in our lives:

- The Holy Spirit teaches and reminds us about the things of God (John 14:26).
- The Holy Spirit dwells in us and fills us (1 Cor. 3:16).
- The Holy Spirit shows us God's thoughts (1 Cor. 2:10–11).
- The Holy Spirit gives us power (Acts 1:8).
- The Holy Spirit guides us into truth (John 16:13–15).
- The Holy Spirit distributes spiritual gifts (1 Cor. 12:7–11).
- The Holy Spirit intercedes for us when we are weak (Rom. 8:26–27).
- The Holy Spirit enables good fruit in our lives (Gal. 5:22–25).

- The Holy Spirit gives us hope that does not disappoint (Rom. 5:5; 15:13).
- The Holy Spirit gives us freedom (2 Cor. 3:17).

Putting It All Together

We could summarize God's stance toward us as demonstrated in Psalm 139:5 by saying God is our ever-present advocate. God is ultimately for us in any and every way possible, as we've already seen from Romans 8:31. God is committed to seeing us walk into maturity, but that's the rub if we're being honest. God's ultimate goal might not align with ours, because God isn't looking to ensure our happiness. Romans 8:16–18 (NIV) shines a light on God's purposes:

> The Spirit himself testifies with our spirit that we are God's children. Now if we are children, then we are heirs—heirs of God and co-heirs with Christ, if indeed we share in his sufferings in order that we may also share in his glory. I consider that our present sufferings are not worth comparing with the glory that will be revealed in us.

There are a few things worth teasing out in this passage. First, we are heirs of God. What a remarkable destiny we have. It's too easy to think about this Christian life as a rescue plan, where Jesus saves us from our terrible sins. But here the apostle Paul says we're not just saved from something, we are saved into something. We are co-heirs with Christ. What a magnificent promise, one that has been fraught with theological concern throughout the history of the church. Is Paul saying we're the children of God in the same way that Jesus is the unique Son of God? Yes, and also no. We're not members of the Trinity like Jesus (this goes without saying, but I want to say it anyway), but we inherit God's grand future as children of God. We too quickly downplay our future.

Second, downplaying our future is exactly why suffering feels so overwhelming and frustrating. We have lost sight of God's grand plan for the future in which we will have full intimacy with God in the new heavens and the new earth. Our eschatological vision stays small, so we allow our struggles to overcome our hope. It's vital to grasp the idea that our tribulations pale in comparison to the future in store for us. Plus, let's compare notes with the apostle Paul real quick. He was stoned, he spent several nights in the open sea, he was bitten by a poisonous snake, he was chased out of town by angry mobs, and so much more . . . and he still says that none of this amounts to a hill of beans compared to the glory that will be revealed in him. If Paul can say this, surely all our problems appear smaller than our future. So we have to be certain we align our hearts with God's purposes, and only then will we be able to step forward in confidence, regardless of what life throws at us. To the degree we can face our struggles directly, to the same degree we will be equipped to help our children handle their struggles.

Engaging Our Kids with This Truth

Life is hard, and to act like it's not is less than honest. Our kids deserve radical honesty about the challenges life can bring. We've been talking about this already in the previous chapters, but here we add one key differentiator that can build tenacity in our children. Beginning to understand the radical commitment God makes to us with the Holy Spirit builds strength and comfort in the reliability of God. Our kids can learn to settle into and trust the character of God as a result of God's gift of the Holy Spirit, and this will inevitably bring increased stability and mental strength to the forefront of their often-tumultuous lives.

Ages Three to Seven

At this age, we can encourage our kids to start thinking about deeper theological truths in a fast and memorable way. We can start with the bullet points above about the Holy Spirit. For each of those characteristics of the Holy Spirit, we can read the verse of Scripture to our kids and ask them to tell us what they think it tells us about the Holy Spirit. From there, we can add a sentence or two describing how this truth applies to their lives, then move on with the rest of our day. Here's an example for you: Read John 14:26 to your children and ask them what they think this teaches them about the Holy Spirit. Encourage them in their answer, then say, "The Holy Spirit teaches and reminds us about the things of God. Does it frustrate you when you forget something important like taking your lunch to school? This means God knows we forget things sometimes, and God will remind us about important things without ever getting angry at us. God never gets disappointed when we forget important things."

There are other creative ways we can engage our younger children with the idea that God is all around and within us. Here's one simple, quick, fun, and memorable way to get their attention on a deep topic. Without any warning or context, ask your child where God is right now. See what they say, and expect an answer like "In heaven" or pointing to the sky, and encourage them no matter what they say, because there's no wrong answer. Then read Psalm 139:5 to them and say something like this: "Do you know what that means? It means God is in front of us all the time. It means God is behind us all the time. And it means that God is upon us all the time. He's everywhere all around us, all the time. That's pretty awesome, isn't it?"

Ages Eight to Twelve

You can use that list of the roles of the Holy Spirit with this age group too, with the additional benefit of being able to engage them more on the topic at hand rather than having a quick conversation and moving on with life. As an example, let's use Romans 8:26–27 and the associated statement that describes it, "The Holy Spirit intercedes for us when we are weak." Start by reading this short passage to your children—preferably in an easy-to-understand version like the New Living Translation or New International Version or a paraphrase like *The Message*—and ask them what they think it means. Be sure to encourage them for any answer they give; this isn't a math class where there's only one right reply, after all. Fundamentally, we want to engage our kids in what the Bible has to say. Ask them about the last time they felt weak or confused. If needed, you can suggest a couple of potential answers like missing lunch and being super hungry or being teased at school by some bullies. Then tell them, "Did you know that you can ask the Holy Spirit to help you whenever you feel weak? You don't even need to know the right words to pray, because the Holy Spirit will translate everything you're feeling and tell God about it. God might even give you strength based on that simple thought you share with the Holy Spirit. Pretty neat stuff, right?"

Another example of how to engage this age group can be by using James 1:17. Read the verse to them and ask them for some examples of good gifts that God has given them recently. Give them time to answer as always, and then suggest a few things that will be relevant to your kids. Examples might include anything from how they scored that soccer goal last week to the new friends they're making in school. Then tell them that every good thing is a gift from God. Too often our kids (and we) will attribute good things that happen to other sources, like our own skills, luck, or karma. But this verse tells us that every good thing comes from our heavenly Father, so we should be helping our children to see their lives that way. We will talk more about the concept of gratitude in the next chapter, but for now, this exercise will get them thinking about how God is all around us and is generous to us.

Ages Thirteen to Eighteen

Again, we will start with that list of the benefits of the Holy Spirit in a believer's life, but we can dive yet deeper still. A great example of an engaging study to have with an adolescent might be with the spiritual gifts, found in 1 Corinthians 12:7–11. For this activity, you'll want to read all the listings of spiritual gifts, so you also need to include Romans 12:6–8, 1 Peter 4:10–11, and Ephesians 4:11. Read these lists of spiritual gifts and ask them if they have any questions about what any of the spiritual gifts look like, then answer those questions for them as best you can. Keep in mind that you don't have to have a master's degree in theology to talk to a teenager about anything related to faith, just be honest with them. Then ask them what spiritual gifts they think they might have been given by the Holy Spirit. Once they're done talking about this, share your opinion about the things they do very well related to spiritual gifts. For example, you could encourage them by saying that they are spectacular servants and really seem to enjoy opportunities to meet others' needs, or you could talk about how they can communicate truths about God in powerful ways. The key is to be specific, honest, and forthright with them. You could even mention something that isn't "on the lists," because many people believe the spiritual gifts lists in the Bible are not complete. Take this opportunity to build up and strengthen your young adult—this will bear great fruit in your relationship with them over time.

ENGAGING WITH YOURSELF

1. How easy is it for you to remember that God is actively working for you, preparing the way for you to travel by going before you? What are your struggles with this if you have any?

2. What is your response to the teaching above about the Holy Spirit being a nonrefundable deposit, where God claims you as his possession?

3. In reviewing that list of benefits of the Holy Spirit, which one stands out to you the most right now?

4. What do you believe your spiritual gifts are?

Verse to Consider or Memorize

*"For the LORD will go ahead of you;
yes, the God of Israel will protect you from behind."*

Isaiah 52:12

God will always act as a forerunner ahead of us. God will prepare the way for us and make smooth the pathways. Even when it seems like things aren't going our way, we can rest assured that God's remains with us through our challenges. And we can be equally assured that our rear guards are protected from unexpected attacks too. We should actively teach our children by engaging them in the reality of the Holy Spirit in their lives and ours. Teaching about the preeminence and presence of the Holy Spirit for believers might be one of the best antidotes to fear from suffering and challenges.

6

WE MUST DEVELOP A RITUAL OF GRATITUDE

"Such knowledge is too wonderful for me, too great for me to understand!"

Psalm 139:6

Engaging with the Bible

King David pauses here in Psalm 139 to recognize how everything he has been saying up to this moment is too amazing to comprehend. The actual creator of the universe knows everything about us. God intimately knows our actions and always sees us. God knows our words before we speak them. What a privilege we have! We are, after all, just little humans with often small dreams living out our sometimes-unremarkable lives as best we can. Yet God spends all this attention and energy on us. With David, we can and should join in a chorus of praise, one born almost out of confusion but also birthed in gratitude. There are two distinct though related concepts about gratitude that we will explore in this chapter: reasons to express gratitude to God and what gratitude builds into us. Both remain vital as we consider developing a ritual of gratitude for our families.

Reasons to Express Gratitude to God

In one sense, you could make the argument that we have unending reasons to express gratitude to God. God has done so much for us and has given so many specific answers to our individual prayers. But it doesn't always feel that way, does it? When days are exhausting, we need to be able to "prime the pump" of praise toward God. When our depression is wielding its ugly scythe in our lives, we might not feel like praising God. When anxiety makes everything feel overwhelming, the last thing we want to do is express gratitude to God for anything. This section will help remind us of the wonderful things God has done for us when everything feels far less than ideal in our lives.

John 3:16 carries within it the foundational reason we should praise God. God has chosen out of his own free will to offer us salvation. This offer isn't based on anything we have done or ever could do; it is an expression of his great love for us. God has longed to have a people for himself from the beginning of time. We can see this in the original creation story, in the calling of Abraham, in the covenantal promises given to the nation of Israel, in the prophetic writings even after the nation was conquered, and finally in Jesus. God has been consistent in his desire to draw a people to himself. So when Jesus offers salvation to all who will come, he perfectly reflects the heart of God.

Another reason to be grateful to God can be discovered in Philippians 4:6–7: "Don't worry about anything; instead, pray about everything. Tell God what you need, and thank him for all he has done. Then you will experience God's peace, which exceeds anything we can understand. His peace will guard your hearts and minds as you live in Christ Jesus." God offers us peace during turmoil. Now, let's tread carefully with this passage, because it has been weaponized by too many pastors who try to "help" those in their congregations with anxiety. This passage does not say that prayer defeats clinical anxiety, because it's not talking about clinical anxiety at all. No, this passage speaks to the everyday worries that can cross our minds and promises that we can know peace instead of worry. When faced with worry (not anxiety), we can lift our concerns up in prayer and God will exchange our worries for his peace. We can partake in this exchange as we learn to trust that God can and will handle our concerns well because God is trustworthy.

A third reason to express gratitude to God is that he protects us. This can be tricky because sometimes bad things happen though we love and serve God, which makes it seem like there isn't protection after all. Maybe we experience a job loss that jeopardizes our family stability or there's an assault on one of our children, and we're left wondering why God didn't show up during this sadness. We must take hold of the kingdom of God theology we discussed earlier in moments like this and continue to place our trust in God.

Psalm 91:1–2 says,

• •

Those who live in the shelter of the Most High
    will find rest in the shadow of the Almighty.
This I declare about the LORD:
He alone is my refuge, my place of safety;
    he is my God, and I trust him.

• •

The promise contained in this passage and many others scattered throughout the Bible says God protects those he loves from harm. This becomes an opportunity for us to be very specific in our gratitude by thanking God for the individual times he protected us from harm. Instead of thinking of God as our protector in a generic way, I can thoughtfully consider, for example, how he kept my family safe while we drove through that poorly lit, strange town in our junky car. We made it home instead of breaking down in the middle of nowhere, and that was God sustaining our vehicle. We all have stories like this that demonstrate the specific protection of God over our lives, and this becomes fodder for praising him.

In 1 Corinthians 15:57, Paul identifies another reason we can be grateful to God when he says, "He gives us victory over sin and death through our Lord Jesus Christ." We can choose to be thankful because we have victory over sin and death. It's difficult to comprehend exactly what it means to have victory over death, because death remains a scary thing to consider, but another part of the Bible speaks to this. First Thessalonians 4:13 says we should "not grieve like people who have no hope." The passage goes on to talk about the resurrection of the dead when Jesus returns, and this is a strong reason to praise God. Our loved ones who are in Christ will be resurrected at the end of days instead of left in some grave rotting forever. What a glorious promise! First Corinthians 15:57 also talks about how we can overcome sin through Jesus. I think of my father, who was a lifelong alcoholic until he met Jesus. In a miraculous moment of freedom, I remember him showing me where he had hidden all the bottles of booze throughout the house and us emptying them together. He said to me, "I don't need the bottle anymore because I have found hope in Jesus!" We have access to this same freedom-making power over sin. Both sin and death have lost their power to control us in Christ.

Another reason to have gratitude toward God is the stability of our relationship with him. Romans 8:38–39 says:

> I am convinced that nothing can ever separate us from God's love. Neither death nor life, neither angels nor demons, neither our fears for today nor our worries about tomorrow—not even the powers of hell can separate us from God's love. No power in the sky above or in the earth below—indeed, nothing in all creation will ever be able to separate us from the love of God that is revealed in Christ Jesus our Lord.

The apostle Paul gives us a pretty good list here of things that could potentially separate us from God's love, but he doesn't stop there. Instead, he adds the phrase "nothing in all creation" to the end of his soliloquy about God's love. Just in case we can think of something that isn't already covered in the other items Paul lists, he included this catch-all. Our loving relationship with God is 100 percent stable and nothing can change that. Period. End of story. No sin, no mistake, no family issue, no demon, no fear, no worry . . . nothing can change the relationship we have with God. This goes against what we can so often think and concern ourselves with. We are quick to think God might become sick of us due to our weaknesses or mistakes, but Romans 8 says otherwise. Nothing will change the degree to which God loves us, and that's praiseworthy.

One final reason to have a thankful heart toward God is that we have an inheritance of eternal life waiting for us. First Peter 1:4–5 states it this way: "We have a priceless inheritance—an inheritance that is kept in heaven for you, pure and undefiled, beyond the reach of change and decay. And through your faith, God is protecting you by his power until you receive this salvation, which is ready to be revealed on the last day for all to see." The Scriptures are strangely quiet on what exactly this inheritance holds for us beyond referring to it as *eternal life*. Nowhere in the Bible do we have a description of what this eternal life will consist of or what we will be doing during our eternal life unless you count the apocalyptic descriptions in Revelation, which might be metaphorical rather than accurate portrayals of how we will spend our time. Yet still, we are left with the promise of God protecting a pure and undefiled inheritance in heaven for us, keeping it safe until we receive it. Scripture tells us that the Holy Spirit serves as a down payment toward that inheritance, so we can glean some things about this inheritance from our interactions with the Holy Spirit. Surely intimacy and connection with God will be part of our inheritance, along with a loving relationship and guidance, only to a greater degree than we currently experience. We can join with the saints of old and praise God for this mysterious inheritance that will be forthcoming in the next life and revel in God's protective power in the meantime.

What Gratitude Builds in Us

If we aren't careful with gratitude, it can start to feel like something we must do to stay healthy in our relationship with God. Whenever obligation enters any relationship, it gets sour, and this is no different with God. Gratitude cannot become an obligation but needs to remain a privilege. While we should be careful not to praise God to get things from him, the Bible is clear that gratitude builds certain things into our lives as we practice it. As a starter, thankfulness centers us on God's will. First Thessalonians 5:18 states, "Be thankful in all circumstances, for this is God's will for you who belong to Christ Jesus." This verse can be difficult to follow because some circumstances aren't easy to find God in. For example, how can we praise God over a cancer diagnosis? I don't have answers to questions like this, but my family has learned to be thankful through our difficulties, and we have learned to trust

God more in the process. Something powerful happens when we trust God in the dark, so to speak, which allows us to feel centered in God like nothing else.

Gratitude also opens pathways to healing for us. In Luke 17, Jesus heals ten men of leprosy and tells them to go to the priests. One returns to Jesus and praises God for his healing. Jesus rebuked the nine others who didn't return and declared that faith healed the one who returned. There's a bit of mystery as to what exactly happened here, because the narrative stated earlier that all ten were healed on their way to the priests. One thing is certain though—the man who returned received favor and healing from Jesus beyond what the other nine received. We must be careful with taking this analogy too far. We can't try to manipulate God into healing by using formulas, because God's healing has no human formulas or predictability. Taking a quick look at the healings that take place in the New Testament makes this clear. Sometimes handkerchiefs heal, sometimes spit heals, sometimes shadows heal, and sometimes people's legs are strengthened as soon as they stand up. There is no pattern and no guarantees. But one thing remains certain: gratitude opens the door to potential healing, and that's a good thing.

Praising God will also build contentment. First Timothy 6:6 says, "True godliness with contentment is itself great wealth." As we recognize the wealth that having intimacy with God brings to us, the allure of material things will fade into the background. We will be content with not having the newest iPhone or Tesla and will find joy in simplicity. There's a common thought that says good Christians shouldn't be wealthy, based, for example, on the passage in the Gospels where Jesus tells the rich young ruler to sell all his possessions and follow Jesus to find eternal life. Yet at the same time, we see that the patriarchs in the Old Testament were by and large very wealthy men and women, so there is a contrast at play here. The key to this apparent contradiction can be found later in 1 Timothy 6:9 where Paul says, "People who long to be rich fall into temptation and are trapped by many foolish and harmful desires that plunge them into ruin and destruction." We should not long to be rich but instead content ourselves with what God has given us. This pattern of contentment comes to the forefront of our lives when we focus on thanking God for what we do have rather than focusing on what we don't have or what we want to have.

Gratitude also teaches us to live in the present instead of the past. Ecclesiastes 7:10 tells us, "Don't long for 'the good old days.' This is not wise." It is far too easy to look to the past and glorify what used to be. This becomes dangerous because it causes us to lose heart for the goodness of the present and to long for what once was. The ironic thing about this longing is that we typically look back on the past with rose-colored glasses as we long for the so-called good old days. We forget the hard times that came with the good and, instead, only remember how great they supposedly were. Being thankful helps us to see that positivity exists in the present. Yesterday remains invariably connected to today, and both have things to praise God for because he is present in our yesterdays and our todays.

Engaging Our Kids with This Truth

Developing a ritual of gratitude is caught more than taught, so we have to do more than conduct a Bible study to help our children understand this truth. It's also true that tenacity is connected to gratitude, because we are growing roots into God's love by centering ourselves in the good things God has done in our lives. While we do need to introduce our children to the concepts discussed above, it's more about regular reminders through modeling that will help them develop this habit in their lives. Because modeling looks much the same for all age groups on this topic, we will not break out the different ages in this chapter. Here are three ideas to help your kids learn to develop an attitude of thankfulness toward God:

1. Verbalize the praises you have in your head when you're around your kids. This might be as small as getting a parking spot near the mall or getting one of the last loaves of bread that were on sale. Instead of letting this go, remember James 1:17 that we discussed above, recognize the good thing that just happened in your life as a gift from God, and say something about it. It can be very simple and short, something like, "I'm sure glad God takes care of us in big and little ways, like giving me this close parking spot." This gets your kids used to hearing praises directed to God, and it coaches you to recognize those moments as well.
2. Develop a daily family ritual of noting where God has done something positive in your life. This can easily be done over dinner or before bedtime, but a couple of things are important about this ritual—you should try to do it at the same time every day, and you want everyone in your family to participate as much as possible. Many families have complex schedules, so it might not be possible to have everyone join in every day, but it's vital to have as many as possible. This helps everyone to see the variety of ways that God's goodness shows up, and it teaches everyone to be on the lookout for God's touch in their day. It becomes especially important to continue this ritual when your entire family or someone in your family is going through a difficult time, because we want to encourage our kids to believe that God remains active even when everything isn't going perfectly. When

we're barely sustaining ourselves or one of our children is struggling, this practice can be a source of encouragement. Even in difficult times, God is moving.
3. Read through one or more of the verses listed in the previous section of the chapter as a family and look to answer the question, what does this verse have to do with gratitude? As always, be encouraging with every answer and generous in your feedback. We always want to encourage our kids to answer, even if their answer seems to be "out in the weeds" from what the Bible verse is saying. With that in mind, dialoguing is much more important than having the best answer. It might also be worth asking, does something in this verse seem hard or unreasonable? This will help our kids to engage with the Bible in a constructive way rather than only looking for proof texts to support their thoughts.

ENGAGING WITH YOURSELF

1. How regularly do you express your gratitude to God for the things he's done in your life? Do any mental health conditions make this more difficult for you in certain seasons?

2. Of the reasons to praise God given above, which do you find the most difficult? Why do you think that might be?

3. What fruit do you see in your life from praising God, and which seems to be missing the most?

4. What's your initial response to the idea of having a daily gratitude ritual with your children, and how do you think they will respond when you start it?

> **Verse to Consider or Memorize**
> *"I bow before your holy Temple as I worship.*
> *I praise your name for your unfailing love and faithfulness;*
> *for your promises are backed*
> *by all the honor of your name."*
> Psalm 138:2

This verse is particularly meaningful to me as it ties God's honor to his promises. We can believe the promises of God because he has proven himself to be faithful in the past, both in our personal histories and throughout the history of the world. God's honor is at stake every single time one of his promises is in jeopardy of not being fulfilled. Whenever it seems like God is absent, his promise of being near to the brokenhearted has the right to be questioned. We even see this in the Psalms and the prophets, where people cry out to God, asking him to remember his name and his faithfulness, to act in accordance with his name. We can do the same—when things aren't going well, we can ask God to show up based on the promises given to us. When we feel abandoned, we can remind God that we have been promised to never be forsaken. God will arise to the challenge of his honor, and while we can't force God into action, we do see God responding to these challenges throughout history.

7

WE CANNOT ESCAPE GOD

"I can never escape from your Spirit!
I can never get away from your presence!
If I go up to heaven, you are there;
if I go down to the grave, you are there.
If I ride the wings of the morning,
if I dwell by the farthest oceans,
even there your hand will guide me,
and your strength will support me."

Psalm 139:7–10

Engaging with the Bible

There are times when we want to escape from God. Whether due to shame, pain, or confusion, we desire most to isolate ourselves from everything and everyone, including God. We want to wallow in our sorrow or stay in our pain. We want to do nothing but stay right where we are, because if we're honest, we feel like nothing will change anyway. The effort and energy to put hope on as a garment can feel exhausting, since we truly believe hope will only disappoint in the end. So we run, we hide, and we hope to never be found by anyone. But the excruciating promise of God says he will always find us. We can go nowhere to escape the presence of God, and this becomes even more true for us as New Testament believers because of the indwelling Holy Spirit. Allow me a little creative license as I reinterpret these verses in light of my personal struggles with mental health:

> If I go up to the heights of a manic episode, you are there.
> > If I go down to the depths of a depressive moment,
> > > you are there.
>
> If I run as far away as I can
> > out of shame for my mental health conditions,
>
> even there your hand will guide me,
> > and your strength will support me.

Mental Illnesses Are Not Sinful

Some people believe mental health conditions remove the goodness of God from our lives, as though God is disgusted by the very idea of any type of mental instability. This comes from a faulty belief that any type of mental health condition is a sin. Since God hates sin, God must, therefore, hate the person who has sin (a mental health condition) within them. This is wrong on multiple levels though. To start with, mental illness is not a sin any more than a broken arm is a sin. These events happen to us for any number of reasons—some based on our choices and some not based on our choices—and they exist as facts in our lives, nothing more. Let me say it more clearly for those who need to hear it directly. Your depression is not a sin. Your anxiety is not a sin.

Your bipolar disorder is not a sin. Your schizophrenia is not a sin. These are events or things that have happened to you, but they don't define you or your relationship with God.

This brings me to the second point of contention. Even if we were sinners because of a mental health condition (which we aren't), God wouldn't hate us. God is not in the business of hating human beings; God loves us. There is a line of reasoning that says we are given the gift of our salvation through Jesus's sacrifice on the cross, but we have to earn the rest of our relationship with God. Based in part on the idea that we should confess our sins to God to restore fellowship with him, it gets mixed up with other bad relational theology and just turns gross.

Galatians 5:1 counters this theology: "Christ has truly set us free. Now make sure that you stay free, and don't get tied up again in slavery to the law." Paul was initially speaking to circumcision as the way to gain God's favor, but it applies equally to any law that enslaves us. Adding anything to the grace of God takes away from the freedom offered in Christ and becomes a false gospel. We are not called into slavery but into freedom, a freedom based on the beautiful sacrifice of Christ for our sins. Paul continues in verses 7–8 of Galatians 5: "You were running the race so well. Who has held you back from following the truth? It certainly isn't God, for he is the one who called you to freedom." Again, we see the call of God toward freedom instead of slavery. This runs absolutely against what the theology of God hating people with sin says and instead offers us full access to our heavenly Father.

Any effort we put toward sanctification or purification should come from the Holy Spirit who dwells within us. Once more, we can turn to the book of Galatians for some insight here, this time Galatians 3:1–4:

> Oh, foolish Galatians! Who has cast an evil spell on you? For the meaning of Jesus Christ's death was made as clear to you as if you had seen a picture of his death on the cross. Let me ask you this one question: Did you receive the Holy Spirit by obeying the law of Moses? Of course not! You received the Spirit because you believed the message you heard about Christ. How foolish can you be? After starting your new lives in the Spirit, why are you now trying to become perfect by your own human effort? Have you experienced so much for nothing? Surely it was not in vain, was it?

The apostle Paul here explains that we can't rely on our strength for support as we grow in maturity toward Christ. Let's bring this full circle. One can hope that depression or anxiety or any other mental health condition might lessen as we draw near to Christ (though that's not always true and it hasn't been true in my own life), but whether that happens or not is not up to our effort. We can't force our mental health conditions to go away by becoming better Christians. It doesn't work that way. The Holy Spirit will be the one who brings about a change in us, or not, according to the Lord's will.

It's important to revisit the parenthetical thought above now. Christian maturity does not mean a mental health condition will lessen or go away. I've been a Christian for over thirty years now and drawing closer to Jesus as best I can, but I have continued to struggle with deep depression throughout these years. Some years have been easier than others, but I've never been without at least a reminder of my depression. Sometimes mental health issues disappear under the grace of God; sometimes they don't. And sometimes we have to do the hard work of healing from past hurts before we can rewire our brains to function better. This perfectly explains the process of sanctification, and it's a long journey.

Philippians 1:6 says, "I am certain that God, who began the good work within you, will continue his work until it is finally finished on the day when Christ Jesus returns." There's a timeline for sanctification hidden in this verse that's easy to miss if we aren't paying attention, but it's a lifelong thing. The verse says God will continue working on us until Christ returns. In other words, there are no shortcuts to perfection. And this is especially true when dealing with a mental health condition, because a mental illness isn't typically a sin that needs to be purified but rather a combination of reactions to trauma, genetics, and learned behaviors. Sometimes it can be overcome through hard work, medication, and counseling, but sometimes it sits unfinished until Jesus returns. We must be okay with this possibility, as heartbreaking as it might be for us.

Heartache is not all that God has to offer us when our health sits incomplete on this side of heaven though. He promises his presence as an unchanging reality for us. As the key verses for this chapter state, there is nowhere we can go that can keep us from the presence of God through the Holy Spirit. This is of course because the Holy Spirit, through one of the great mysteries of our faith, dwells within us as Christians. This means running from God is equivalent to running from our elbows—it's simply impossible.

Beyond his presence, God offers support, strength, and help. The Bible contains many verses we could point to in support of this concept. Hebrews 13:6 tells us: "We can say with confidence, 'The LORD is my helper, so I will have no fear. What can mere people do to me?'" It's important to consider the phrase "mere people" here in our context of mental health, because we are "mere people" too. In other words, even we ourselves can't keep God from helping us. This isn't to say that we have no say in our lives. On the contrary, it declares the grandeur of God's great love for us that outstrips even our fear of somehow disqualifying ourselves from God's goodness.

Engaging Our Kids with This Truth

This is the first time in this book we've directly addressed any theological claims about mental health conditions, and that's on purpose. There is more to stronger mental health than having or not having a mental health issue, but it would be foolish to ignore the concept entirely. This is particularly true in light of the growing number of preadolescents and adolescents who have been diagnosed with mental health conditions. If one of your children is struggling with his or her mental health, you simply must address this topic head-on without shying away from it. We must communicate to our kids at every age that God isn't disappointed in them because of a potential mental health condition, God isn't ashamed of us when we battle these circumstances, and God isn't going anywhere. Establishing this reality for our kids can help them develop tenacity as they settle into a more complex but unmoving relationship with God.

Ages Three to Seven

With this age group, it's unlikely we will be dealing with mental health conditions, so we might not need to talk about what God thinks of mental illnesses necessarily. That being said, if your youngster is battling mental health issues, by all means jump into this conversation. In many circumstances, we can instead invest heavily in our kids and the way they think God thinks about them. My pastor once said, "What we think about when we think about what God thinks about us is the most important thing we can think about." That's a mouthful, but there's solid truth there. We want to give our children every chance to learn that God desperately loves them, no matter what comes up in their lives. Here are three great ways to work with younger children to help them understand that God's love for them is unconquerable:

1. Dramatically read Romans 8:38–39 to your kids from *The Message* paraphrase of the Bible. Ask them if they've ever wondered if God would stop loving them over something they've said or done and remind them (as always) that there's no wrong answer to this question. Once they've answered, assure them that even that thing can't keep God's love from them. The Bible specifically says that absolutely *nothing* can get between us and God's love. Remind them that Jesus is giving them an enormous hug right now, even though they might not be able to feel it. Then give them a tight hug and say, "Jesus is hugging you just like this, every day, all the time. He never gives up on us, period."
2. Summarize the parable of the lost sheep for your kids by saying this: "In Luke 15, Jesus tells a great story about how much love he has for every single one of us. He compares himself to a shepherd who lost a sheep, one of one hundred sheep that he's watching over. This shepherd leaves all the other sheep to find the one that's been lost. When he finds the sheep—and he keeps looking until he does find that lost sheep—he gets super happy and tells his friends to celebrate with him. That's just how much God loves us. Even when we get lost by making a mistake or sinning, God chases after us until we are found, and then God celebrates with the angels when we're found."
3. Summarize the parable of the lost coin for your kids: "Jesus tells a story of a woman in Luke 15 who lost one of ten coins. She looked in every corner of her house,

swept under the rug, and moved all the furniture until she found it. Then she invited her friends to celebrate with her once she found it. Have you ever lost something really important to you? What did you do to find it? How did it feel once you did find it again? God loves us so much that he keeps looking for us whenever we're lost, and God celebrates once we're found. That's how important we are to God and how much God loves us."

Ages Eight to Twelve
Peer pressure and social expectations start to hit by this time, and it shows in the increasing rates of depression and anxiety within this age group. We might think a fourth grader shouldn't be dealing with depression, and in a perfect world, that would be true, but this isn't a perfect world. Our kids are struggling from younger and younger ages, and we have to step into the gap to help them understand how to cope with these challenges. Reminding them or teaching them that they are loved by God, as discussed above, is a good start, but it's not enough. We have to address head-on the idea that depression or anxiety shouldn't be reasons to feel shame in any way. Here are two different ways to approach this topic:

1. Read Romans 8:1 aloud and ask your children what it means that there's no condemnation. They might not know what the word means, and if they're not sure, that's okay. Give this simple definition: condemnation is what you feel when someone tells you you're not good enough. If needed, repeat the question: What does it mean that there's no condemnation? Be patient as they think through this, because it might be a complex question for this age range, but they should eventually be able to come up with something. Once they have an answer,

add a few of your thoughts to the conversation. Consider saying that it could make a person feel more confident because God says we are good enough, and God is the one who knows best. Encourage your kids to think about this every time a negative self-thought comes up. Ask them what types of negative thoughts they've been battling lately. Your kids might not be ready to talk about this, so don't force the issue, but stay open to how they might respond. If they do give you an answer, remind them that Jesus says there is no condemnation and that the condemning thought isn't true. If they mention depression, sadness, or anxiety, make sure to affirm that it's okay to feel those feelings and that nobody judges them for feeling them. Then encourage them to remember that even in these moments, there remains no condemnation in Jesus.

2. Start a direct conversation with your children about depression and anxiety by asking them, "Do you have a hard time with depression or anxiety? How about any of your friends?" If you have noticed anything with them that makes you wonder if they're struggling with depression or anxiety, mention it in a nonjudgmental way and ask about it. Ask them if they've ever considered what God thinks about anxiety and depression and listen carefully to what they say. Once they're done sharing, tell them that God never judges anyone for a mental health condition. He doesn't expect people to "get better" because they get older or more mature. Instead, he stands by their side, supporting them through thick and thin. If you battle any mental health conditions, share some of your stories here in an age-appropriate way and show them that God hasn't abandoned you in your

struggles. End your time by reading Psalm 139:7–10 and pointing to how we can't escape God, no matter where we go.

Ages Thirteen to Eighteen
Depression and anxiety are at epidemic levels in adolescents, and we have to treat it as the danger it is for our kids. We shouldn't assume our children aren't struggling with mental health conditions because they seem to have everything together. Depression and anxiety are called silent killers, and it's easy to hide them from everyone. Even parents. The best approach to this epidemic is direct interaction on the topics, but we want to reverse the order of the conversation from the younger children. Instead of starting by asking them if they or their friends battle anxiety or depression, we will start by asking what they think God thinks about mental health conditions. This primes the pump and gets your adolescent talking in the abstract instead of jumping right into a difficult conversation. If your kids are anything like mine, once they start to open up, it's like the floodgates open and they won't stop, but the trick is getting them to start. This question hopefully opens the proverbial floodgates.

Ask them if they've ever heard a pastor or church leader say anything negative about depression or anxiety, and ask how that made them feel. What a great opportunity to share what God truly feels about mental health conditions, following the same patterns as mentioned above—God does not abandon those who struggle. God doesn't expect us to "just get better," and he doesn't believe the answer to serious mental health problems is only prayer or Bible study. Then ask them if they are struggling in any way with their mental health, including any observations you might have about their actions lately. Dialogue openly and patiently with them about your battles with mental health if you have any and talk about how God never discarded you as damaged goods. Ask them if you can close your conversation with a prayer over them, and then ask God to fill them with a clear mind and a focused devotion to Jesus.

ENGAGING WITH YOURSELF

1. When was the last time you wanted to hide from anyone and everyone, including God?

2. Have you ever had a pastor or other Christian leader tell you that mental health conditions are sinful, and how did you react to that assertion?

3. What is your response to the idea that God might not "heal" a mental illness on this side of heaven?

4. How difficult is it for you personally to believe that there is no condemnation in Christ, and how do you find success in this?

Verse to Consider or Memorize

"So now there is no condemnation for those who belong to Christ Jesus."

Romans 8:1

This is one of the most powerful verses in all of Scripture. It tells us that we are free from the power of condemnation in our lives. It tells us that we can ignore all the other voices that say we don't measure up, that we aren't good enough, or that there's something wrong with us. Armed with the truth from this passage, we can stand against the darkness that comes at us during our mental health episodes and we can know that God still loves us. Allow this truth to settle into your soul.

8

DARKNESS IS LIGHT TO GOD

*"I could ask the darkness to hide me
and the light around me to become night—
but even in darkness I cannot hide from you.
To you the night shines as bright as day.
Darkness and light are the same to you."*

Psalm 139:11–12

Engaging with the Bible

There are echoes here of what we spoke of in the last chapter. There are moments when we want to hide ourselves away because of the curveballs life has thrown us. Our mental health might be in the dumps, or our kids seem like they're not in a good headspace, so we lose hope that things will get any better. I love how the NIV translates these verses because it captures what we're thinking in these moments:

> If I say, "Surely the darkness will hide me
>   and the light become night around me,"
> even the darkness will not be dark to you;
>   the night will shine like the day,
>   for darkness is as light to you."

This translation shows the desire of our hearts when all seems lost. We say to ourselves (for we believe nobody else listens, after all) that we can hide in the dark. We say to ourselves that light will become night around us. We desperately want to give up and give in to despair, in other words. This is precisely where God steps into the fray. God doesn't wait until we have our lives together to show up, but he also doesn't force his way in. God will let us sit in our self-proclaimed hiding space if that's what we desire, even though darkness is the same as light to him and he can see us and find us in that night.

Let's be clear about something before we go any further though—I'm not saying that anyone who is in a difficult place finds themselves there because they refuse to respond to God. This is a toxic lie that has been perpetrated by far too many well-meaning pastors and Christian leaders, and it does nothing but harm those who hear it. Depression, anxiety, and every other mental health condition are far too complex to be able to say definitively that any one particular thing causes them, especially when that one thing is as subjective as being open to God. Rather, we must be willing to let God in or there is no possibility of his being able to engage with us. God won't show up uninvited, pure and simple. But we should never try to gauge whether another person is open to God working in their lives or not—it's unfair, unreasonable, and often ends up being mean-spirited. Instead, we have the privilege of offering the grandness of God's goodness to those who are struggling by proclaiming to them that God can find them even in the thickest night. This is some of the most profound imagery we can find in Scripture about the character of God, particularly as it applies to us when we are having a difficult time.

First John 1:5–7 has much to add to this discussion:

> This is the message we heard from Jesus and now declare to you: God is light, and there is no darkness in him at all. So we are lying if we say we have fellowship with God but go on living in spiritual darkness; we are not practicing the truth. But if we are living in the light, as God is in the light, then we have fellowship with each other, and the blood of Jesus, his Son, cleanses us from all sin.

God is the very definition of light. We are familiar with him being equated with love, but we don't hear much about him being light. This means God's very essence is light; he is light through and through, and by definition, he cannot have any darkness in him. It would be like André the Giant saying he was a little person—it just wouldn't make any sense at all. We as Christians can't live in spiritual darkness if we desire to be in complete fellowship with God, but what exactly does it mean to live in spiritual darkness? In an unsurprising contrast, John says we are in darkness if we aren't in the light, and he goes on to tell us two specific ways we live in the light in the following verses.

First, John says we need to have fellowship with one another. If we find ourselves living apart from Christian community, it's far too easy to let isolation warp us in ways we aren't even aware of. This has been profoundly true in my life, and after my suicide attempt, I had to decide to engage honestly with trusted people about my mental state. This fellowship protects me from getting out of whack mentally or emotionally because I am investing in relationships with people who know me well enough to know when I'm not my best self. The same is true for all of us—we must be in fellowship with other like-minded, trustworthy people to keep us safe from ourselves. Second, John says when we live in the light, we keep short accounts of our sins before God. Again, I'm not equating mental illness with sin, so let's not confuse things. We all have issues of sin that we deal with though—uncontrolled outbursts of anger, lust, gossip, the list goes on. John says we need to bring those things to God and allow the blood of Jesus to cleanse us from our sins. Then we are walking in the light of God.

But what about when we do all the right things and still feel like we're stumbling around, unable to see anything? We're in committed friendships that keep us safe and we have short accounts of sin with God, but we still feel all alone and bereft of God's presence. This is when we, like King David, must strengthen ourselves in the Lord. We can read of a desperate situation in which David found himself in 1 Samuel 30. The Amalekites had burned his stronghold and taken his wives and children along with those of his men. The men wept until they could weep no more and then threatened to stone David because his decisions had led to this terrible outcome. This is when we read that David strengthened himself in the Lord. From there, he sought a specific direction from God and acted on this direction. As a result, he and his men caught up to the Amalekites, vanquished them, and restored their families.

While we don't know precisely what David did to strengthen himself in the Lord, we can still learn a lot from this story. He came to God from a place of total desperation, fear, and dependence. He was grieving because his family had been stolen from him, and he was afraid for his life because of the threat of being stoned. Then he sought and received guidance from God on what to do next. We can do the same. We can come to God when there's nothing left to even hope for and cry out, *What now God?* And he will answer us. Like David, we will be able to chase our Amalekites and regain what the enemy has taken from us.

Psalm 56:3-4, a psalm written by David, comes to mind in times like this: "When I am afraid, I will put my trust in you. I praise God for what he has promised. I trust in God, so why should I be afraid?" We are quick to put our emphasis on being afraid, on our circumstances, on our mental health conditions, or on the fact that God hasn't done anything to pull us out of our difficulties. But that's not the emphasis in these verses. David focuses on the fact that he *will* put his trust in God and praise God for his promises, despite not seeing evidence of them being fulfilled in that moment. David chooses to praise God in advance, amid chaos, because he knows the character of God. And it's not just fear to which we can respond this way. In his life, David was angry and disappointed and despondent and irritated and many more things; yet in most of these situations, we see that he turned to God. In contrast, we often deny that we feel afraid (or any other emotion) and put a spiritual spin on it somehow, as if being emotional is shameful. Then we choose not to deal with our emotions or declare our presumptive trust in God's character despite what we see. Instead, we sit in our unexamined emotions and do nothing. God calls us to do more.

Engaging Our Kids with This Truth

The topics covered in this chapter might be the most important material in the book when it comes to coaching our children toward tenacity. I guarantee that hard times will come for them; they will hit hard, and they will come more often than we want them to come. If we don't start talking with our kids now about how to bounce back when things go awry, then they may very well shipwreck their faith. But, to take a positive spin on things, it's possible to begin talking with our kids about God being light at any time. We can instill in even our youngest children the idea that God is a light in the darkness, but we also need not worry that we've missed the boat if our kids are older. It's never too late to begin conversations about God's light shining in dark places. We want to have these conversations, ideally, before a tough time comes. Then our kids will be prepared ahead of time with the coaching and theology we've been sneaking into their hearts, and they will be better prepared to weather the storms. The best time to start this conversation is yesterday, but the second best time is today.

Ages Three to Seven

Here are two ways to approach the topics discussed in this chapter with younger children:

1. At the dinner table one evening, ask your kids if they've ever felt like God didn't show up when they expected him to. As they're thinking about this, give an example of a time in your life when this happened, keeping it age appropriate. It could be a time when you were really sad and God didn't fix your sadness, or maybe a time when something bad happened to you that you feel like you didn't deserve and God didn't do anything about it. Make a couple of suggestions of things that might be true in their lives, such as a friend starting to ignore them or a teacher being mean for no good reason. Don't force them into an answer, and tell them it's okay if they can't think of one. Either way, tell them that God promises to never leave us alone in the world. Read part of John 14:18 to them, showing them that it's a promise

from Jesus. "I will not abandon you as orphans." Ask them if they know what the words *abandon* and *orphan* mean and give definitions if needed. End the time by saying that Jesus promises he will always be with us, even if it doesn't feel like it.

2. Take your kids into a walk-in closet and turn off the lights. If you don't have a walk-in closet, get everyone under a heavy blanket and turn off the lights. As you sit in the dark, ask them if they're afraid at all. If they say yes, ask why they are afraid since they know they're at home and with you. If they say no, ask why they aren't afraid. Then keep talking to them about nothing for a few minutes. Ask them if they know where you're at, even if they can't see you. Ask them how they know, to which they will either say "I can see you" or "I can hear you." If they say they can see you, ask how they'd know where you were if there wasn't any light, and they should say they would be able to hear your voice and follow it to where you are. Tell them it is the same with God, that we can listen for his voice even in the dark, and God will sometimes tell us what to do. Then turn on a flashlight (you can use your phone for this) and ask them if they can see now. Once they say they can see, tell them that the Bible says, "Your word is a lamp to guide my feet and a light for my path" (Ps. 119:105). This means that one way we know what God wants us to do is to read his Bible, and it will show us the types of decisions God wants us to make. The Bible won't tell us about every decision to make, but it will certainly help guide us so we won't feel like we're so alone.

Ages Eight to Twelve

It would be appropriate to use either of the above scenarios for older children, with some slight modifications. If these don't feel like good fits for your children, then here's another way to approach teaching the concept of following God in the dark and God being light:

After dark, set up an obstacle course in your house while your kids aren't in the room. Make it pretty complex, where it won't be easy to guess your way through it without some help. Turn off all the lights and bring the kids into the room, then tell them to navigate through the room(s) without hitting anything. Don't give them any guidance or any help (or any flashlights) to do it, and just listen as they struggle through it. Make sure to mix in a few comments when you hear them bounce off chairs, like "Oh, it sounds like you hit a chair. Be careful!" Keep it lighthearted instead of aggressive, as this might frustrate your kids, and you don't want to add to their aggravation. At some point, they might want to quit or they will get through the room; there's no pressure to finish the obstacle course. Tell them that they will do it again but with a slight difference this time.

This time, they will close their eyes tight and follow your voice. If you prefer, you can tie a bandana around their eyes so they won't be tempted to look. You can use a flashlight to guide yourself, because otherwise, it would be a real disaster. Give them very specific directions to guide them through the obstacle course, like "Take two small steps to the right." Finally, bring them back to the front of the room again and take their blindfold off (or tell them to open their eyes) and give them the flashlight. Tell them to go through the obstacle course on their own.

Quiz them a bit about their three experiences. Start by asking which was the hardest and what made it so hard. Then ask whether it was easier to have the flashlight or listen to your voice, and ask them why. Note that there's no right or wrong answer to this question—it's a matter of opinion, though we can expect that holding the flashlight would be the easiest. Then tell them that Psalm 119 says, "Your word is a lamp to guide my feet and a light for my path." Sometimes life feels like an obstacle course in the dark, but there are at least two ways we can find our way through without bumping our knees and tripping over everything that's in the way. We can listen to someone else give us directions. Sometimes, those directions will come from God through his Holy Spirit directly to us, and sometimes those directions will come through the kindness of other people, like parents or pastors or teachers or friends. We can also use a flashlight. The Bible is like a flashlight when times get tough, because it tells us what types of decisions God wants us to make. It won't give us the answer to every single question, but the Bible will give us a lot of help when we are struggling.

Ages Thirteen to Eighteen

The best thing to do at this age is to talk it out. Playing games with flashlights isn't going to impress a fifteen-year-old, so we need to just not go there. Instead, ask your kids point-blank if they've ever been disappointed by something God didn't do for them. As they think about this and how to answer, provide them with a very serious answer from your own life of a time when you felt abandoned by God. Talk about how you overcame this feeling of aloneness and retained your faith, being brutally honest about whatever that process looked like. If you walked away from the faith for a few years, tell them that. Don't pull any punches in your story, because your kids deserve to know the truth. As they share their experiences with you of feeling left by God, don't be too quick to give them a spiritual answer about how we can know that God promises to always be with us. Instead, dwell with them in their pain and commiserate with their story. It's vital here that you avoid diminishing their experiences in any way, such as stating that their story doesn't sound that tough or that they should have been able to power through that circumstance.

Transition to a quick Bible story. Tell them that you're going to be hanging out in John 6, but that you promise not to read the whole chapter to them. Instead, summarize the story for them by saying something like this: "One time Jesus spoke to the crowds, and he said some crazy stuff that didn't make sense to most of the people following him. He said anyone who wanted to be his disciple had to eat his flesh and drink his blood. We can look at this and understand that he's referring to what we now call the Eucharist or Communion, but the people first listening had no way of knowing this. So they stopped following him because it got weird. Jesus turned to his disciples and asked if they were going to leave him as well. Peter answered Jesus and said they weren't going anywhere because Jesus had the words of eternal life."

You can then go on to discuss that sometimes in life, we have to trust in the character of God even when what he's doing doesn't make sense. That's what the disciples did here; they chose to trust in Jesus even when what he said seemed ridiculous. They trusted what they knew about Jesus from spending time with him instead of reacting to his current actions. When things get tough and it seems like God stays absent, we have to do the same thing. Instead of believing what we're seeing with our eyes about God, we must lean into what we already know about him. Then ask, what are some things you know to be true about God right now, today? Remind them to do their best to remember these things that they know to be true now when they are struggling. This is the key to staying close to God when he doesn't seem to make any sense.

ENGAGING WITH YOURSELF

1. What is your initial response to the idea that God is light and his presence ushers darkness away? When has this been true in your life?

2. What do you think it means to strengthen yourself in the Lord as David did?

3. How difficult is it for you to place your faith in God by choice when your emotions start to get the best of you? What strategies have you uncovered to help you do that?

4. Have you ever had a John 6:68 moment, where it seemed like God wasn't making sense, but you chose to follow him anyway because of what you knew about him? What was that like?

> ### Verse to Consider or Memorize
> *"Lord, to whom would we go?*
> *You have the words that give eternal life."*
> John 6:68

When things go sideways, this is a great verse to be able to recall. This is a verse that will remind you that God is good and kind and generous and life-giving. Even when it feels like he's nowhere to be found, we can trust in what we already know to be true about him. We must build up our trust in him when times are good so that when we face tough times, we can be prepared with a personal history with God to battle the temptation to walk away from him. We must remember that Jesus has the words of life.

9

GOD KNOWS OUR BROKEN PARTS AND STILL LOVES US

"You made all the delicate, inner parts of my body and knit me together in my mother's womb."
Psalm 139:13

Engaging with the Bible

God stitched us together and has known us from the very beginning. God knows every inch of our being. God knows the way our middle toe has grown slightly longer than the toe right next to it, which makes our spouse chuckle. God knows the way our hair does that weird thing whenever it gets too long. God knows that our left knee sort of snaps like we're at a chiropractor if we sit still for too long. Nothing about our body surprises God. But God's knowledge extends beyond physical characteristics too. God knows if we tend to get nervous before going on an airplane despite the statistics that say we will be safer flying than driving.

God knows how agitated we get when someone bad-mouths our spouse and how we want to lash out at that person. God appreciates how a baby coo makes us smile, every single time. Nothing surprises God about who we are.

This also includes the broken parts of who we are, and that can be very intimidating. Some Christian circles say we have to have all our stuff together before we can come to God, because he is holy and expects the same of us. This thought is based on verses like 1 Peter 1:16, which says, "You must be holy because I am holy." But this verse is taken out of context and, therefore, removed from its original purpose. Let's together consider 1 Peter 1:17–21 to gauge the true message of this passage:

> Remember that the heavenly Father to whom you pray has no favorites. He will judge or reward you according to what you do. So you must live in reverent fear of him during your time here as "temporary residents." For you know that God paid a ransom to save you from the empty life you inherited from your ancestors. And it was not paid with mere gold or silver, which lose their value. It was the precious blood of Christ, the sinless, spotless Lamb of God. God chose him as your ransom long before the world began, but now in these last days he has been revealed for your sake.
>
> Through Christ you have come to trust in God. And you have placed your faith and hope in God because he raised Christ from the dead and gave him great glory.

There's a lot to unpack in this section of Scripture. It starts with the very uncomfortable idea that God will judge us according to what we do, rather than playing favorites. At first glance, this might feel like a "works righteousness" passage, where God decides what to do with us based on what we've done for him. Everybody would be in trouble if this were the case; but thankfully, that isn't the message of these verses. We will be judged based on what decisions we make about Jesus Christ. If we decide to allow Jesus to be the king of our lives and accept his sacrifice as our Savior, then we are gifted the righteousness of Jesus. This is the path through which we can attain for ourselves the holiness that God embodies. There's no way we could ever arrive at a God level of righteousness through our efforts, so nobody would get to move toward intimacy with God.

When 1 Peter says God plays no favorites, it reminds me of Cornelius coming to faith in Christ in Acts 10. If you remember, God sent an angel to Cornelius to send for Peter to talk to him about Jesus, and then God gave Peter a vision to prepare him to go talk to this gentile (Jews weren't in the habit of visiting gentile homes for fear of making themselves unclean according to Levitical laws). Peter went to Cornelius's house and began to preach the good news about Jesus. While he was still speaking, the Holy Spirit fell upon everyone listening, so Peter baptized them, and they became part of the fledgling Christian movement. As part of his preaching, Peter said he realized God does not show favoritism to anyone but welcomes all. Almost certainly, Peter thought about Cornelius as he penned these words in his letter, and that's very instructive to us. As Christians, we can be confident that he has brought us into the family of God, and we don't have to worry about being accepted into his future kingdom. This runs counter to the message of holiness, which says we have to earn our way into God's heaven.

But Peter has more to offer us in this passage. He goes on to say we must live in reverent fear of God. It's important to remember this as we consider the fact that God knows everything about us. Before we go any further, it's important to talk about what it means to have a reverent fear of God. This does not mean we should be afraid he will strike us down with lightning if we don't meet his standards. That's an unhealthy fear and not what God calls us to have. A reverent fear recognizes that God is the creator of all good things, is greater than us, and is utterly different than we can ever hope to be. We can and should come into this relationship with an overwhelming sense of gratitude and a recognition that he is different from us. This combination creates reverent fear in us.

It is the otherness of God that speaks to the reality that God knows everything about us. It would be impossible for us as humans to know everything about another person and not have that influence our view of them. Think about your spouse or a close friend—you allow your knowledge of them to guide the way you view things that happen in your relationship with them. You assign motives to them based on who you know them to be. And sometimes you get their motives wrong because you inappropriately assume motives that don't exist. God never does this. He never assigns improper motives, because he knows us perfectly. He doesn't misrepresent what we're trying to accomplish when we do or say something. We can trust God with our hearts because he has always been fundamentally trustworthy. We should allow confidence to well up in our hearts even as we consider those dark corners of our lives that aren't fully sanctified. We talked earlier about how sanctification is a lifelong process, so God doesn't expect us to have everything together.

What about living as temporary residents—what does that have to do with God recognizing our broken parts and still loving us? We denigrate ourselves so quickly with statements like this: "I'm just a sinner saved by grace" or "I'm only trying to do my best, and some days it seems like that's not very good." God knows our destiny, and that destiny surpasses these negative statements by a long shot. God says we are called through Jesus Christ to something far grander than just surviving and doing our best. We used to have empty lives, as Peter puts it, but now we are called to more. Galatians 4:7 puts it this way: "Now you are no longer a slave but God's own child. And since you are his child, God has made you his heir." Ponder that for just a moment. We are heirs of God. Everything that belongs to him, belongs to us. If God had a last will and testament, we would be in it, and we would be receiving everything. That's a remarkable future and demonstrates that God has remarkable trust in us.

Our role is to live up to this inheritance made available to us rather than living down to our previously worthless lifestyles. It is a hard word to say that our lifestyles are or were worthless, so let's unpack this a little more to see if we can soften the blow. Peter says we inherited an empty life from our ancestors, but what exactly does that mean? I think it's a pretty complex topic, but we can understand it with some relevant thoughts from today. If the end goal of our lives is to finish with the most toys or to further our family line through children, is that really worth all the heartache? Does it make sense that we are seemingly surrounded by struggles, failures, and mental health conditions if the end is just death? I think not, personally. It's all too difficult for material goods or the honor of our family. Particularly for those of us with mental health challenges, it's just not worth it. It feels impossible to live up to the high calling of being God's heir in Jesus Christ, because this world is so hard.

I can't sit here and tell you that it will be easy to step beyond these struggles, but it's possible. I am a testimony to this. A few years ago, I couldn't see beyond my depression, and I was very distant emotionally from God. I was going through the motions of my faith but couldn't connect with God because of shame. I knew the Bible, but its power was lost on me because I was so tied up in personal battles. One day, during a stay at a mental health facility, I heard the Holy Spirit whisper to me, "I still love you." I argued with him because I didn't know how God could still love someone as messed up as me. I was sitting in a mental health facility following a suicide attempt, and I didn't even love myself. How could God love me? He didn't engage me in the argument though. He just repeated himself. "I still love you." This broke me in the best of ways. I realized I could never make a mistake that would take me beyond the reach of God. God knew the broken parts in me and loved me anyway.

This connects with the last few verses in our 1 Peter passage. God paid a price to rescue us from our formerly worthless lives, and it was a high price indeed. It wasn't gold or silver but the precious blood of his Son Jesus, the perfect Lamb of God. If God went to such great lengths to establish a relationship with us, what in the world could pull us out of that relationship? Romans 5:10 says it like this: "Since our friendship with God was restored by the death of his Son while we were still his enemies, we will certainly be saved through the life of his Son." In other words, there is nothing that can sever the relationship that has been established through the blood of Jesus. We have become friends and heirs of God through this sacrifice, and nothing will change that. Nothing we do, nothing we say, and nothing we think can change this powerful truth.

Engaging Our Kids with This Truth

Too often, Christian leaders will communicate to other believers that it's only once we're cleaned up that God will really love us fully. The language is never that direct, but the insinuation is clear. And it's harmful, especially when it's our kids hearing these unbiblical concepts and internalizing them. One of the keys to a biblical form of tenacity is to know in the deepest part of ourselves that God is fundamentally and irrevocably for us, always. This will lend us and our children strength in weakness and courage in despair. As usual, the specific ways we introduce these concepts to our kids will differ based on how old they are.

Ages Three to Twelve
Tell your kids that you are going to do something sort of weird today, and that it might be hard for them to do it, but that you'll go first to help them out. Ask them to think about something they aren't proud of about themselves or don't like about themselves. As they're thinking about how to answer that question, you answer with something either you aren't proud of or happy about now or something you used to not like about yourself. This could be anything from having to wear glasses to the color of your hair. Try to keep it sort of light instead of going with something really heavy like body image, unless you believe your kids will be more engaged with a tougher topic. Explain what it is you didn't like, why you didn't like it, and even if you were teased at all about it. Then ask them to share the thing they don't like or aren't proud of about themselves. Listen intently and ask incisive questions to really get them talking about this thing, whatever it is.

Shift gears in the conversation by asking them what they think God thinks about the thing you didn't or still don't like about yourself. Expect them to either be positive toward you or to say, "I don't know." Regardless of what they say, though, be encouraging and try to get them to talk more about it. Ask why they aren't sure or why they think positive things about what you thought or think of as a flaw, again always encouraging them for any answer. Then ask them, "What do you think God thinks about your thing that you don't like about yourself?" They might stammer or get flustered, and if they do, don't sit in the awkward. Tell them, "I have some thoughts about that thing. Can I tell you what I think God thinks about that thing you don't like about yourself?" Assuming they say yes, respond with something like this: "God knows every part of you inside and out, and he loves all of you. Even those things you don't like, God knows and likes. Even with your habits that frustrate you, God sees them and loves you. There is nothing you can do that would ever cause God to lose interest in you or love you less."

Ages Thirteen to Eighteen
This conversation will be somewhat like the one with the younger children but with a few twists along the way. You will start with the same question: What is something they aren't proud of about themselves or don't like about themselves? Give them some time to think about this by sharing a story about something you currently don't love about yourself or aren't proud of. You will have to trust your kids to carry your burden here, but go deep with the example you give about yourself. Talk about your body image issues or how you wish you were more motivated to exercise more or the way you sometimes fib when you're pressured. Be transparent about things you are currently struggling with and talk about how they affect your relationship with God. Perhaps you wonder if God gets fed up with you and your issues. If that's you, talk about it. It might be an emotional moment for you, but push through and share anyway. Remember, you have a purpose for sharing difficult things here—you are modeling something to your children.

Ask your kids to share the thing they don't love about themselves or aren't proud of. If they pick something shallow, gently push them to dig deeper as you did with your story. Listen intently and ask probing questions as they talk about this thing that disappoints them about themselves. Encourage them as they share that you don't think any less of them and to keep digging deeper into why they are ashamed or unhappy with this thing in their lives. Once you're satisfied they've talked enough about it to enter the next part of the conversation, ask them, "What do you think God thinks about the problem I've shared with you? Does he think less of me because I'm struggling?" Tell them you're not looking for false encouragement and that you struggle with these feelings sometimes—you're not looking for them to be your therapist, but let them know you'll take seriously anything they say to you.

Now turn the table on them and ask, "What do you think God thinks about that thing you're not proud of or don't love in your life?" Promise them you won't give them any cheesy Christian answers as you interact with them, and ask them to be honest about their answers. Listen carefully and ask reflective questions as they bare their hearts to you about this struggle they have. Be careful to not give any answers right away but instead engage in drawing them out more and more into the open, gaining their trust along the way with supportive questions.

Once it seems like they've shared what they're willing to share, respond to them with something like this: "I promised that I wouldn't give you any cheesy Christian answers, and I'm going to keep that promise. These are hard topics we're discussing, and it's not easy to believe that God doesn't give up on us. Especially when we're making mistakes and we know that God is perfect. But here's the thing—God doesn't expect us to be perfect. God is far more interested in seeing us move in the right direction than in seeing us stop making mistakes. God knows we're all works in progress and gives us grace along the way as we grow and mature. Here's a Bible verse for you to think about. Romans 5:8 says, 'God showed his great love for us by sending Christ to die for us while we were still sinners.' Think about this for a moment: If God sent Jesus to die for our sins when we were a total mess and had nothing to offer him, why would God step away from us now? He wouldn't, and he won't. God knows we're still messed up, and he loves us anyway."

ENGAGING WITH YOURSELF

1. How difficult is it for you to accept that God knows all the dark recesses of your heart but still loves you?

2. What does it mean to you to live in reverent fear of God?

3. What does the phrase "temporary residents" mean in your daily life?

4. What is one thing right now that you're ashamed of or not proud of when it comes to your walk with God, and what do you believe God would say to you about that thing?

> ### Verse to Consider or Memorize
> *"Fear of the LORD is the foundation of true knowledge, but fools despise wisdom and discipline."*
> Proverbs 1:7

We can only grow in our understanding of God by accepting this reverent fear of him as the foundation of our relationship with him. It's far too easy today to think of God as a friend or a lover, and these are important concepts, but we must never forget how other than us he truly is as well. This verse tells us the fear of the Lord is the beginning of wisdom, for only in understanding our relationship with God do we find our true selves.

10

WE ARE EXTRAORDINARY

"Thank you for making me so wonderfully complex!
Your workmanship is marvelous—how well I know it. . . .
How precious are your thoughts about me, O God.
They cannot be numbered!
I can't even count them;
they outnumber the grains of sand!
And when I wake up,
you are still with me!"
Psalm 139:14, 17–18

Engaging with the Bible

We thank God for many different things, but I can't think of the last time I thanked God for me. I don't often thank God for his marvelous workmanship in creating me. That feels somehow outrageous or prideful, but we see it right here in Psalm 139. Let's practice this for a moment or two and consider our grandeur. Here's a list of things that just work, and they may seem as miraculous as they seem mundane, because we take these things for granted:

- Our eyes translate the images we see into meaningful pictures, and our brains assign values to those pictures in words we have learned so we know we're looking at a beautiful sunset when we see it.
- Once we learn to walk (barring injury), we don't forget how to do it. Our legs work, one in front of the other, every day without us even having to think about it.
- Our hands remember how to grasp spoons to eat cereal, how to type from the home keys on a keyboard, and how to tie our shoes.
- Our hearts beat and we breathe and our eyes blink and we swallow, all without putting forth any effort or even a thought toward them, yet we would die if these things weren't happening.
- We remember our parents every time we see them, even if it's been too long since the last time, their hair is grayer, and there are more wrinkle lines on their faces.
- We know how to laugh when we're happy, we can cry when we're sad, and God has placed within us the capacity to be both.
- When we look through our high school yearbook, we often recall the friends and the emotions and the things that happened like they were yesterday, no matter how many years have passed.
- We can translate the words on a page like this one into meaning, whether it's a recipe to make pancakes or a book that encourages us in our faith in God.
- We can do our jobs well, whether that be as a parent, an accountant, a salesperson, or a plumber. We can conduct all the tasks necessary to perform that job with excellence and efficiency, some without even needing a second thought before finishing them.

The list could go on forever, but this serves as a good start. The psalmist says he knows well the way God's workmanship is marvelous, but I wonder how well we know it today. God created something wonderful when he created us, and every day proves the majesty that is us. It's too easy to get caught up in the everyday activities of life and forget how remarkable being a human is, and it's just as simple to get lost in our dysfunctions and forget what works well for us. What a powerful exercise to consider all the things that go right every day for us to be able to function, one that will stir up a sense of praise toward God for his amazing, meticulous creativity. Our primary identity is as a creation of God. As God breathed life into Adam and Eve in the garden of Eden, so he created us. We pull away from this idea because we understand the scientific realities undergirding this truth, but God made us. God formed us and is worthy of praise because of this wondrous creation.

Taking time to praise God for ourselves is a worthy exercise for two reasons. First, we develop a fresh gratitude for the goodness of God that's evident in our lives every single day, almost hidden in plain sight. Second, we gain a healthy appreciation for ourselves. Instead of focusing on all the things we don't do perfectly, we can see the things that work well, the things we perform well, and the things that are perfect. This will be a breath of fresh air in an often stale and discomforting world that expects perfection.

In Psalm 139:17-18, David goes on to talk about how precious and innumerable God's thoughts are about him. On its face, this also feels obnoxiously arrogant. "O God, I know how much you're thinking about me because I am such a wonderful person. You have no choice but to think about me, since I'm so great." But a closer look at the Bible tells us David had grabbed hold of something true about God. Throughout Psalms, we see how God stays almost obsessed with thinking about humanity. Psalm 115:12-13 says, "The LORD remembers us and will bless us. He will bless the people of Israel and bless the priests, the descendants of Aaron. He will bless those who fear the LORD, both great and lowly." We talked about fearing the Lord in the last chapter, so keep in mind this includes us. The Lord will remember and bless . . . us. God consistently thinks about us, how to bless us, and how to move in our lives.

The New Testament adds more to this imagery. Ephesians 2:10 says "we are God's masterpiece." Other translations use the word *workmanship*, but I am enamored with the use of the word *masterpiece*. Think about the nuance of this word for a moment from the perspective of the creator of the masterpiece. Imagine God as a painter, and God has his masterpiece in front of him. God knows it's a masterpiece and is proud of what's been created. There's no doubt in God's mind that something special has just been created. God knows it's his best work.

And there's something else that's true of a masterpiece too—it's never hidden in a closet. No, the artist is proud of his work and wants to show it off. He wants everyone to see it because he knows it's amazing. Imagine God thinking about us in this way, and you are walking on holy ground. In my book *Perfectly Abnormal: Uncovering the Image of God in Chronic Illness*, I wrote the following: "We are God's Sistine Chapel. We are to God as *The Marriage of Figaro* is to Mozart. If God were Bono, we'd be *Sunday, Bloody Sunday*. We are worth everything to him."

We don't spend enough of our lives thinking about ourselves as God's masterpiece, and we don't coach our kids to do that either. Instead, we are too busy living life as it comes at us, doing our best to get through each day unscathed. But God calls us to step beyond the daily grind and recognize who we are. If we can learn to live as God's masterpieces, it will dramatically affect the way we view ourselves, the way we respond to critical moments in our lives, and the way we allow others' words to influence us.

We will stop viewing ourselves as unfinished and will recognize that God knew what he was doing when he created us. We will no longer denigrate ourselves for every little error we make and will instead recognize that being a masterpiece doesn't mean mistakes won't happen. We will learn to look at ourselves with the same eyes of grace that God has for us. We will take joy in the things we do well rather than ignore them and focus on those things with which we struggle.

The critical moments in our lives will still be stressful. When depression raises its ugly head, we can stand firm, whether that depression takes hold of our spirits or not, and know that God doesn't judge us for being depressed. If anxiety pops up, we don't have to worry about God thinking less of us if we succumb to it. This doesn't mean we don't have to work hard or put forth our best efforts, but we can have confidence that God will be for us and on our side because we are his masterpiece. This will lower the stakes somewhat, because we won't have to worry about pleasing God every second to gain his approval. We already have God's approval, and nothing can change that.

The words of others will carry less weight in the grand scheme of things because we know who we are and whose we are. Instead of needing to strive for the approval of every person who "matters," like our bosses or our girlfriend's parents, we can rest in the knowledge that the most important person in the universe has already accepted us. Beyond accepting us, God loves us. More than loving us, God is proud of us and calls us his masterpiece. This changes things.

Engaging Our Kids with This Truth

We are going to approach all age groups with the same activity in this case because the conversation can be valuable for all age groups. Start by telling them that Ephesians 2:10 calls us God's masterpiece and ask them what that means to them. Explain how masterpieces aren't accidents—they come from a lot of diligent work, and the artist is proud of their work once they're done. Make sure you spend a lot of time explaining this term, because the idea of a masterpiece is key to this activity. For younger kids, you might need to stay here awhile to make sure they understand its significance. This means God shows us off to the angels and whoever else will listen because he's that proud of us.

At this point, it's easy to imagine one of your kids sarcastically saying something like, "Yeah sure, God's work is amazing. Then why am I such a mess all the time?" Don't correct them if this happens, but instead engage them in a conversation about it. Ask them why they feel like they're such a mess and what they think God thinks about them and their messes. Encourage them by explaining how they aren't always a mess and that God sees good things in them. Then transition to a slightly different conversation.

Tell your kids you are going to do an experiment, one that could be a bit frightening to both them and you. But you'll go first to make it a little less scary for them. Then tell them that they have to participate or this will be super awkward and hard. Have the following three questions written down on a piece of paper, which you hand to them. If your children cannot read yet, you can read the questions aloud instead:

- What do I (Mom or Dad) do well?
- When you think of me, what do you think of?
- What do you think God is proud of me for?

Instruct them that they need to answer these questions about you in as much detail as possible. Especially with the first two questions, the answers don't need to be spiritual in any way. They can say you make dinner well almost every night, and that's a great answer. Help them tease out answers without making it forced or uncomfortable, then tell them it's their turn to be on the hot seat. Answer the same questions about your kids, being as generous and as honest as you can be. Keep in mind, again, that the answers to the first two questions don't need to be especially spiritual. If your kid makes a great taco, say that—it counts. But think carefully ahead of time about the third question. This is a tremendous chance to build faith into your children's lives that can be beneficial for years to come.

I had the privilege of teaching some of this material to the youth group at my church, including the idea that we are God's masterpieces. After having a youth leader sit in the "hot seat," I invited members of the youth group to come and have their peers speak good things about them. The depth, transparency, and forthrightness of the answers honestly surprised me. There were some silly answers, like saying one young man was great at being teased. (If this happens with your kids, don't immediately shut down the silliness; it's normal to respond to serious questions with a bit of lightheartedness. At the same time, especially with that third question, be ready to push a little bit for a serious answer. It can be as simple as, "I'm sure you have a more serious answer than that. Let's hear what you've got.")

In that youth group, the answers inevitably turned sincere and serious when we got to the third question. Teens were telling each other that God was proud of them for sticking it through some tough mental health challenges or for being an excellent friend who never fails to be there when it counts. Many tears were shed that night, by both leaders and youth. I had a member of the youth group come up to me two months later at church and thank me for that exercise because the words she heard that night got her through some difficult times in the subsequent eight weeks. Something profound and life-changing occurs when we invest intentionally in other people's spiritual lives, especially children and young adults. They take these words to heart and remember them. We can create moments that will build tenacity into our kids' lives, and this is one of those moments. Step into it with courage and see what God will do with it—I can almost guarantee you will be surprised.

ENGAGING WITH YOURSELF

1. When was the last time you thanked God for yourself, for your body and the miracle it is? What did that stir in you when you did it?

2. Do you feel like God is thinking about you often? Why or why not?

3. What emotions do you feel when you hear you are one of God's masterpieces (pride, disbelief, astonishment, confusion)?

4. What is something for which you believe God is proud of you? Why do you think he's proud of you for that thing?

> **Verse to Consider or Memorize**
>
> *"We are God's masterpiece. He has created us anew in Christ Jesus, so we can do the good things he planned for us long ago."*
>
> Ephesians 2:10

We've discussed this a little bit already, but it's worth revisiting. God states in unequivocal terms that we are his masterpiece. God is proud of what he sees when he looks at us and wants to show us off to anyone who will pay attention. What a tremendous reassessment of our identity for most of us, because we live in a world that tears us down. It's also an opportunity to help our kids grow in their understanding of God's great demonstration of love for all of us. God didn't just call us masterpieces, though. He created good things for us to do. These things he wants us to do are distinctly perfect for us to accomplish based on who we are, what we have gone through, and what we bring to the table in our relationships with others. In other words, we can reach people and do things that nobody else can because of what we've gone through.

Don't hear me wrong here, though. I'm not trying to say the truly evil things that may have happened in your life need to be redeemed by God in some way. My childhood abuse wasn't necessary for me to be "used by God" in the future. That theology minimizes the pain evil things cause in our lives. What I mean to say is that our experiences are often the catalyst for meaningful connections with others who have gone through similar pains.

11

GOD KNOWS ALL OUR DAYS

*"You watched me as I was being formed in utter seclusion,
as I was woven together in the dark of the womb.
You saw me before I was born.
Every day of my life was recorded in your book.
Every moment was laid out
before a single day had passed."*
Psalm 139:15–16

Engaging with the Bible

It's hard to imagine God taking the time out of what must be a busy schedule to watch us being formed in the womb. He does have a universe to run, after all. Why would God take the time to invest in watching our little bodies being formed into cohesive human beings anyway? We've already spent a lot of time talking about the tender spot God has in his heart for humans, and specifically for you and me, so we won't revisit that here. Suffice it to say, God's love for us compels him to have a grand interest in us, even before we've demonstrated anything like a passing interest in him. After all, if we aren't even born yet, we can't exactly decide to follow Christ.

And then the verses go on to say that God knows every day in our lives from the beginning until the end, knew them before the beginning had even started. This brings up so many questions worth discussing, both for our own understanding and for our kids. Goodness knows at some point they will start asking questions on topics like this, and we better be prepared with some answers or they will begin to lose interest in their faith and start calling it irrelevant. Let's start with the biggest question of all: Does God know everything that's going to happen to us, the good and the bad? If so, why doesn't he stop the bad things from happening? It seems like God should stop all the bad stuff from happening if he's the good and all-powerful God he appears to be in the Bible. So, what's the deal?

Before we can answer those questions, we have to get a bit technical in this chapter, but we'll also bring it back to practical matters and conversations with our kids. First, we have to lay some theological groundwork. We need to start with one very interesting idea, that of God's eternal nature. Isaiah 57:15 identifies God this way:

> The high and lofty one who lives in eternity,
>   the Holy One, says this:
> "I live in the high and holy place
>   with those whose spirits are contrite and humble.
> I restore the crushed spirit of the humble
>   and revive the courage of those with repentant hearts."

We could camp out on the idea of God restoring the crushed in spirit and reviving repentant hearts, but that's for a different book.

Here, I want to emphasize the way the prophet Isaiah defined God at the start of the verse. Isaiah called God the high and lofty one who lives in eternity. When it says he inhabits eternity, it means he is outside of or, perhaps better, above time. Time is irrelevant to God because he does not live in time as we do. This is a very difficult concept for us to understand because we do live in time and can't imagine living outside of or above time, yet this is what Scripture tells us about God.

Eternity becomes the only way we can make sense of what we read in 2 Peter 3:8, where it says, "A day is like a thousand years to the Lord, and a thousand years is like a day." It would be easier to understand this if only the second part of the statement were there, because that would simply mean God has been around for a very long time. Then it would be like when we hear our grandparents talk about how time flies as we get older. But we don't have just the idea that a thousand years is like a day; we also have the opposite, that a day is like a thousand years. Now, we can draw parallels to this as well from our own lives. We've all had days that seem to drag on for "an eternity," like the day before we leave for a vacation. But God isn't looking forward to a vacation, and he's not talking about time flying because he's getting older either. No, this must be something entirely different. This is referring to the idea of eternity, and it's asserting that time is irrelevant to the way God works.

But God's eternal nature does not mean he is a deterministic God who has ordained all the things that will happen in our lives, reducing us to mere pawns who perform acts decided eons ago by the master planner. God believes wholeheartedly in the free will of men and women on this planet and leaves a portion of the future open to the possibilities of what will occur based on the choices we make. This is why we see God regretting the decisions he has made. For example, in Genesis 6:6 we read that God regretted creating humankind because they were acting with such evil intent. This was what caused him to flood the world and kill all life except what was in Noah's ark. We see another example in 1 Samuel 15:11, where God says, "I am sorry that I ever made Saul king, for he has not been loyal to me and has refused to obey my command."

If God were a deterministic God who sat enthroned on high, separated from everything, and knew the end from the beginning in all things, how could he have regret? To have regret, there must be some element of surprise at the way things have turned out. As a silly example, nobody would buy a broken-down car on the side of the freeway from the owner and then regret that it wasn't running for the simple reason that they would already know it wasn't a good vehicle. In the same way, God must have needed to see how events would unfold to learn the hearts of men or he would never have had any regrets over his decisions.

Similarly, we see God discovering things throughout the Bible, and this doesn't make sense if God already knows the outcomes of all things. From the very beginning, God involved men and women in the orchestration of events. We can see this in Genesis 2:19 when God brought all the animals to Adam to see what he would name them. The sense of the word translated as "to see" is one of discovery, with the underlying concept being that God didn't know Adam would call a giraffe a giraffe, as one example. Later in Genesis 22, God tests Abraham's faith by asking Abraham to sacrifice Isaac as a burnt offering. It would be cruel and unusual punishment from God if he already knew the outcome of the test. What would be the purpose of testing Abraham in such a dramatic fashion if God already knew the outcome?

In Judges 3:4 we read, "These people were left to test the Israelites—to see whether they would obey the commands the LORD had given to their ancestors through Moses." If God knew what the test would reveal, why put the Israelites through the trials unless God is a vindictive and cruel God? Perhaps the most enlightening example of God testing someone can be found in 2 Chronicles 32:31—"When ambassadors arrived from Babylon to ask about the remarkable events that had taken place in the land, God withdrew from Hezekiah in order to test him and to see what was really in his heart." This verse outlines the purpose of all the testing God puts various people and nations through. He wants to see what is really in a person's or a nation's heart, and that's only demonstrated by how they act. Since God isn't an arbitrary or vicious or mean-spirited God, then the best explanation of his testing throughout the Scriptures is that he legitimately doesn't know how people will respond. God can see the potentialities of how they could respond but remains uncertain of what their actions will show about their hearts at the moment.

This brings us full circle to the question of why God allows painful events to happen in the first place. God believes wholeheartedly in the free will of men and women and won't interfere in their choices, even if those choices bring calamity upon them. God will provide opportunities or tests for individuals so he can see their hearts through their actions, but God will never superimpose his will on another person to accomplish his purposes. This is where it gets complex, because it's not just our own choices that affect us; other people's choices have an impact on us too. Sometimes we experience pain because of our own poor choices, as a consequence of sin if you will. Other times we experience pain because of the poor choices of others who are directly in our lives, such as with child abuse. We haven't done anything to "deserve" these things, but another person's poor choices have directly impacted our lives. And still other times, systems in the world that are run by powerful men and women or corporations make decisions that create misfortune in our lives. If we find ourselves working for too low a wage to provide for our families, systems created that misfortune. It's not anyone's fault directly, but the world's systems are sideways and broken by sin, which affects us.

It can be challenging at best to maintain a positive mental state amid such difficulties. It appears God's hands are tied by God himself, and he won't help us when he could. To an extent, there's some truth to that sentiment, but it's also grossly simplifying things. If God were the type of God who interfered with free will, then we would have an entirely different world altogether. We would be automatons instead of human beings, the cross of Christ would have been unnecessary, and we would not know even the simple joys of choosing what outfit to wear today. There is no middle ground here. Either God honors free will or he doesn't, and both have consequences.

Engaging Your Kids with This Truth

Sometimes we find ourselves scared to address the difficult parts of the Christian faith with our children, but it is exactly these conversations that will help them to develop tenacity. Let's be honest—life is going to feel like an attack on our kids at some point, a mean-spirited joke from a dastardly fiend. If we don't start engaging our children with these complex ideas about God, then they will be left with a staid faith that lacks relevance. This is a setup for failure, and we owe our kids better. We can intentionally interrupt life with some complex topics about God to insert some tenacity into their growing faith.

Ages Three to Seven

There are many things about God that we won't understand, and this is a good opportunity to remind our kids of that fact. There are two different ways to approach some of the core concepts that we covered in this chapter:

1. Ask your children, "Do you know what the word *regret* means?" If necessary, explain that when you regret something, you wish you hadn't done it. Give a simple example, like how a child might regret touching a hot stove after being told not to touch it by their parents. They would regret it because it caused them pain. After this explanation, ask your kids if they've ever done something they regret (surely they have, right?). If they are struggling to think of something, give a simple example from your past, like when you sassed your parents on one occasion and got in trouble for it. Once they've shared their story, ask them about the pain they had as part of their regret, if they didn't already share that. Emphasize to them that pain is a key part of regret. Then ask them, "Did you know God sometimes regrets the decisions he makes too?" Tell the story of King Saul in a couple of sentences. Talk about how King Saul started off obeying God but eventually stopped doing things that made God happy. Add in that King Saul lost the right to be king because of his bad decisions. Encourage your kids to make decisions they won't regret, but also remind them that literally everyone, even God, regrets their decisions sometimes.
2. Ask your kids, "Did you know that the Bible says, 'Every day of my life was recorded in your book'? That means God knows everything that could happen in our lives even before we do. That's pretty cool, isn't it? It means God isn't ever surprised by anything that happens to us. Even the really hard or really sad things, God knows they are coming. He is what's called eternal, which is a fancy way to say that he knows the beginning and the end all at the same time. Imagine picking up a book you were just

starting to read, but you already knew the ending and everything in between before you even opened the book. That's what it's like to be God. We can trust that God will always do what's best for us, even if it doesn't make sense to us at the time and it's confusing. Can you think of a time when something made you sad or confused and you wondered where God was? Let's talk about that time. Maybe together we can sort of figure out why God would allow that thing to happen."

Ages Eight to Twelve

There are ways to discuss complex topics like eternity in meaningful and age-appropriate ways that will get your kids thinking about these topics. And they must start thinking about why bad things happen to good people if there's a good God, because this eventually becomes one of the big questions that cause people to walk away from their faith. Preparing them to think about it now, even if bad things aren't happening to them, will prepare them intellectually and spiritually for when those questions stir up in them due to bad circumstances.

Ask your children what their favorite television show is and why. Get them talking about the show for a bit and show real interest in this topic along with them. If you watch the show with them, add details that you enjoy about the show. Then ask them how it might feel to know the end of every episode before it even started. You might get different answers here, ranging from happiness that they can enjoy the show more by knowing the end to disappointment that they don't get to experience the show in full.

Dial into the latter idea, of being disappointed that they can't experience the show as it's happening because they already know the end from the beginning. Then introduce the concept that God lives outside of time, and that some people believe he knows the end from the beginning like with the television show. Other people believe God doesn't know how we will respond to circumstances until we act. Ask them which they think would be more exciting, and which they think makes more sense for God. Admit that it's confusing to figure this stuff out and read Isaiah 55:9 to them: "For just as the heavens are higher than the earth, so my ways are higher than your ways and my thoughts higher than your thoughts." Then suggest that we don't even know where heaven is, so we have no idea how far heaven is from earth . . . and that's the point. God's ways and thoughts are so different from ours that we don't even know where to begin to appreciate the differences. End the conversation with a brief prayer thanking God for being so different from us and higher than us in every way.

Ages Thirteen to Eighteen

If you and your kids haven't watched the first season of the Marvel television show *Loki*, watch it with them as an introduction to the idea of multiverses, different universes that exist based on the different potential choices people make. In this fascinating show, the Time Variance Authority exists to protect the timeline, to make sure multiverses never occur. Through a series of events that take place in *Loki*, the timeline shatters and many multiverses come into existence. Once you've watched the show with your kids, ask them what they think about the idea of multiverses. Do they think a multiverse type of situation could ever exist, and do they think the Time Variance Authority or something like it could be real? They'll probably laugh at you because it's an absurd question, but point out to them that God exists outside of time.

Maybe a Marvel television show isn't your cup of tea. It's okay, superheroes aren't for everyone. Not to worry, there's more than one way to address this topic of eternity with your teenager. Here's an alternative. Draw a straight line across the middle of a piece of paper. On the left side, write *Creation*; on the right side, write *End of Time*. Ask your teen to list off a few things that have happened in history, anywhere in history, and do your best to place them reasonably on the timeline you've created. Ask them to include a few things from the future, too, even maybe uncertain things like when they get married. Explain that, as humans, we experience time as it comes at us. In other words, creation comes before World War I, and their wedding comes after their birth. There's no other way for us to understand time because we are in it. God, though, is above time. Draw something representing God on the paper above the timeline here, then say, "God experiences all of time at once because he is above time. He sees creation and World War I and your wedding all at the same time. This is what it means to be eternal. It doesn't just mean you live a long time. It means time isn't relevant to you."

Here is one other option for you to talk with your teen about the concept of eternity. Ask your kid how it would feel to wake up every day and already know what was going to happen during the day. They would know what questions were going to be on every final already. They would know who was going to ask who out to prom. They would even know the best answers to give their parents to get out of weird conversations like this one. Would they enjoy having a leg up on the competition, so to speak? Or would it take the joy out of their days if they already knew how everything was going to work out?

Read Isaiah 57:15 to them: "The high and lofty one who lives in eternity, the Holy One." Explain that eternity means to dwell outside of or on top of time. In other words, God doesn't live from day to day as we do. Being outside of time means God could potentially see the end from the beginning. God might be able to see all the potential decisions we could make and know which decision we will make, and we could even say God is like the Time

Variance Authority. He might be protecting the perfect timeline by using his power to make sure the best or right decisions are made by everyone. Ask your kids what they think about this idea. Again, they will probably think it's a silly idea but try to tease it out with them on a serious level if possible.

Introduce the idea that God learns more about us by testing us to see what we will do. Read 2 Chronicles 32:31—"When ambassadors arrived from Babylon to ask about the remarkable events that had taken place in the land, God withdrew from Hezekiah in order to test him and to see what was really in his heart." Suggest that God does the same in our lives, that he will withdraw at times to see what's really in our hearts. Ask them whether this idea of God learning what's in our hearts by withdrawing seems different than the Time Variance Authority approach to God and ask them which makes more sense to them. Remind them that no explanation of God is perfect because God exists beyond our full understanding.

Ask your kids whether they've ever wondered if God was testing them with a particular set of circumstances, and dive into that conversation a bit. Ask questions like this:

- Was it frustrating to wonder why God wasn't jumping in to help you?
- What would you have liked God to do in this situation?
- Did it make you mad that you couldn't sense God when things got rough?
- What, if anything, did you learn from that circumstance that has helped you now?

ENGAGING WITH YOURSELF

1. Have you taken for granted the idea that God dwells in eternity and knows everything? How does the information in this chapter change your perspective on God?

2. How weird does it feel to you to consider that God can regret and God can learn things about us by testing us? Do you think God regrets letting you fall into any mental health conditions you might have? Why or why not?

3. What circumstances have you had where you wonder if God might have withdrawn himself from you to test you and see what was really in your heart?

4. Does it seem to you like God has tied his hands behind his back by choosing to not violate our free will? Would you prefer it if God didn't honor our free will so much but instead stepped in and established good things? What problems might that create down the road?

> ### Verse to Consider or Memorize
> "The LORD God formed from the ground all the wild animals and all the birds of the sky. He brought them to the man to see what he would call them, and the man chose a name for each one."
>
> Genesis 2:19

We are so quick to underestimate the importance God places on us and the type of decisions he places in our hands. This is just one example of the value God places on humanity in general, and that trust extends to each of us individually. Think about it: God had just created the entire earth and all the creatures on it, but he didn't name a single creature. Instead, God brought the animals to Adam one by one for him to name them. God didn't know what Adam would name the animals until after the fact. God could have chosen the names and informed Adam of them, but instead, he invited Adam into the act of creation. God does the same thing today with us. He invites us to participate with him in what he is accomplishing in the world. Indeed, this has been God's plan from the very beginning, to find a people who will join him in his work in the world. Today, as members of the church, we are part of that people. Let's not shrink back from these opportunities to join God in his work but instead lean forward in anticipation for what God might do next, with our help.

12

WE CAN BE EMOTIONAL

"O God, if only you would destroy the wicked!
Get out of my life, you murderers!
They blaspheme you;
your enemies misuse your name.
O LORD, shouldn't I hate those who hate you?
Shouldn't I despise those who oppose you?
Yes, I hate them with total hatred,
for your enemies are my enemies."

Psalm 139:19–22

Engaging with the Bible

These verses seem to come completely out of nowhere and smack us in the face with unexpected emotion. We have no context for these declarations against the wicked, but instead, David appears to simply erupt with rage. Before these verses, enemies and smiting and murderers and hatred don't make any type of appearance in the chapter at all. Indeed, the psalm overall has a tone of tenderness and generosity about the loving-kindness of God toward us. So where does the vitriol come from, and what are we supposed to do with it in our lives?

The most important comment I can make about these verses is that we have permission to be emotional. Many Christians believe having any anger at all is a sin, but that's not the message we find in the Bible. The clearest teaching on this topic can be found in Ephesians 4:26 (and Ps. 4:4), which says, "Don't sin by letting anger control you." We all know the difference between being angry and letting anger control us. What a scary loss of control rage induces when it causes a person to lose their inhibitions and act out of their worst intentions, without thinking about the ramifications of their actions. Rage is what God wants us to avoid. Being angry in the first place isn't a sin.

We can and should look to the life of Jesus as our best example of how to manage our emotions in general. If emotions were looked down upon by God, then we would expect to see an unemotional Jesus, one who operated out of his intellect all the time. Instead, we see a deeply emotional man. Jesus wept, he was moved with compassion, he became angry, he felt sorrow, he was overwhelmed by his circumstances, and more. Indeed, Jesus might be one of the most emotional men we see depicted from the ancient world, and that should give us pause. What does the emotionality of Jesus, alongside his sinlessness, communicate to us about the role of emotions in our lives? At the very least, it banishes that terrible thought too many churches teach that says emotions are, by default, negative things we must manage. Beyond that, the emotionality of Jesus tells us there is a path to godly emotions. No longer do we need to believe the lie that says the most spiritual way to react to our circumstances is to reason through them, ignoring and mistrusting our emotions. Particularly in light of the sadness depression causes, these toxic lies can add burdens to an already struggling soul. If you're that struggling soul, let that lie go and hold fast to the idea that your emotions aren't sinful by default.

When life feels unfair, it's not unreasonable for us to become angry or grieve that unfairness. Perhaps this is what David does in these verses. Certainly in other places we see that David and the other psalmists engaged in grieving and angry responses to injustice. The technical term for this is lament. Lament is rarely brought up in church circles today, despite its prevalence in the psalms. There is a dearth of understanding of why lament can be a powerful part of our faith and what laments accomplish in our journey with God. Instead of acknowledging lament, American Christianity pushes us to stay in a place of happiness or contentedness in our walk with God, even when trials overwhelm us and we need an outlet. Sadly, poor discipleship about the purposes of lament removes a powerful tool from the hands of people struggling to reconcile their belief in an active God with their experience of a life bereft of his presence.

Perhaps even more disturbing, laments can be seen as equivalent to complaining to God or are even viewed as sinful expressions of faithlessness. Nothing could be further from the truth, as an examination of one of the personal lament psalms will prove. Psalm 13 says the following:

> O Lord, how long will you forget me? Forever?
>   How long will you look the other way?
> How long must I struggle with anguish in my soul,
>   with sorrow in my heart every day?
>   How long will my enemy have the upper hand?
>
> Turn and answer me, O Lord my God!
>   Restore the sparkle to my eyes, or I will die.
> Don't let my enemies gloat, saying, "We have defeated him!"
>   Don't let them rejoice at my downfall.

> But I trust in your unfailing love.
> I will rejoice because you have rescued me.
> I will sing to the Lord
> because he is good to me.

· ·

Each lament has four elements to it: an address to God, a description of the complaint, a request for God's help, and an expression of trust in God. These elements can be traced through Psalm 13 very easily. David opens the psalm by addressing God in verse 1 and moves directly into his complaint: he feels forgotten and in anguish because his enemies have victory over him. Then in verses 3–4, he requests God's help, asking God to "turn and answer" by renewing his energy so he doesn't fall to his enemies. Verses 5–6 establish David's trust in God's goodness, despite nothing having changed in his circumstances.

Usually, the complaint to God stirs discomfort in today's Christians. We ought not complain to a God who's been so generous to us, the thought process goes, so therefore, it must be a sin to complain. Some even point to verses in the Pauline epistles that say not to complain, like Philippians 2:14, as proof that this type of lament must be at least flirting with sin. But if we're honest, we all have complaints to lift to God about things not going our way, and sometimes these are quite large events that have turned against us. Like David, perhaps our lives, our livelihood, or our reputation is at stake, and God appears to do nothing. What should we do in these circumstances, if we are not allowed to make our complaints known to God? In the right context, complaints to God are not sinful at all but represent a defiant exclamation of faith in God despite the circumstances.

By moving directly from a description of the complaint to a request for God's help, we prove that we know where our help comes from in dire situations. We know we cannot trust in money or power (today's chariots and horses), but we must rely instead on the God who is always for us. Combine this immediate request to God for help with the equally immediate declaration of trust in God, and we can begin to see how lament serves a deep spiritual purpose. Nothing has changed in the circumstances between when we serve the complaint up to God and when we preemptively thank him for taking care of us, and yet everything has also changed. We have reestablished our trust in God despite the situation in which we find ourselves, and we arrived at this place through the process of lament.

Only by giving voice to our complaints to God can we uncover the faith to continue to trust in God regardless. Lament and true complaining are very different events. For example, think of the Israelites in their desert wandering. Every time Moses turned around, the nation complained about not being in Egypt. They wanted meat to eat. They were thirsty. Hungry. Hot. The list goes on and on, and it exasperated both God and Moses. There was no faith component being established by the Israelites in their complaints. There were no declarations of trust in the goodness of God. No, they rebelled against the goodness of God despite all his provisions for them and his obvious presence in the pillars of cloud and fire. The Israelites wanted to separate themselves from God and return to slavery instead of experiencing the freedom God had in store for them in the land of Canaan.

This contrast between Israel and the psalms of lament underscores one of the purposes behind laments—to praise God. It seems counterintuitive to say a lament that includes a complaint could be praise, but every lament psalm ends with a declaration of trust in the character and goodness of God. Laments call God to act based on his character and his declared goodness toward us. While spoken in the minor key of suffering, laments nevertheless serve as anticipatory praise about the good deeds God will perform on our behalf.

In this way, lament can be a powerful antidote for fear. Through lament we remind ourselves that God is for us, as the apostle Paul declared in Romans 8:31. We stir up our own faith by lamenting because we call God to act in accordance with his nature, and this forces us to consider his nature. By considering God's nature, we are drawn to the goodness and consistency of his character. This recognition of God's goodness and love makes fear dissipate, because perfect love casts out fear. As we ruminate on the nature of God, we can't help but be reminded that God looms much larger in scope and power than whatever problem we might be facing.

And yet lament can do even more in our lives. Lament becomes a pathway to greater intimacy with God. We know God is listening to our prayers, which is the core of a lament, a prayer to God. As he listens to our prayers, we can draw near to God as a result. James 4:8 says if we draw near to God, he will draw near to us, even if that drawing near occurs through lament. We pour our hearts out to God, hoping against hope for a changed life. In the process of doing this, we draw near to him and allow him to return the favor. Oftentimes, laments don't modify the circumstances but do greatly change how we see things because God has drawn near and sheltered us in his cocoon of grace. Grace changes everything.

Lament also invites us to participate in the pain of life with others. As we engage in reading the lament psalms, we may discover that we don't directly relate with the experience of being hemmed in on all sides by enemies, but this could be a daily experience for the underground church in Southeast Asia. By finding and making these connections with the church at large, we permit ourselves to enter another's pain. There is something redemptive about entering another's pain. After all, Jesus was doing just that when he quoted Psalm 22 on the cross, entering the pain of many of the Jewish martyrs of his day.

So, lament is something entirely different from complaining about life not going our way. When we choose to lament, we engage in an ancient practice of recognizing who has the power to change our circumstances and we call God to act on our behalf because of his great love for us. We encourage ourselves and lift ourselves up in faith based on God's anticipated provision for us. We choose to draw near to God by sharing our innermost struggles with him, trusting that God will be gentle with our pain. And we enter the pain of others by lamenting alongside them in their difficult circumstances. Lament is a powerful weapon indeed, and one often underused.

Lament can be particularly useful in the context of mental health conditions. So often our mental illnesses don't simply go away, and at times they even seem to gain strength for no good reason whatsoever. This can create in us a distortion of reality in which our health conditions seem bigger than God. Lament reorients our view of God and puts him in his rightful place as the biggest part of our lives, despite what circumstances might be telling us. In this way, lament restores a modicum of sanity to a moment when sanity is much needed and missing by reminding us that God is good, God is bigger than our problems, and God is faithful to answer our prayers. Even when he seems far off.

Engaging Our Kids with This Truth

Lament is a powerful tool in our tenacity toolbox, and it's worth exploring with our children, no matter how young. Lament gives us permission to be emotional, which is good because everyone is emotional sometimes. Lament can also serve to corner our fear, hemming it in by faith and transparency with God. When we create opportunities for our kids to better interact with laments, we will be coaching them to manage the inevitable trials that will come in their lives and giving them the tools to stay mentally strong when things go sideways.

Ages Three to Twelve
Read Psalm 13 to your kids from *The Message* paraphrase. Ask them if they've ever felt like it's been long enough, like God has ignored them for long enough. For the really young, it might be more realistic to ask them about how it feels to be ignored by their mom or a teacher or a friend when they have something important to say. Encourage them to talk about how it felt to be ignored and ask good questions to tease out the details of that moment. If they don't have anything, be sure not to pressure them into an answer. Instead, share a time from your own life when you felt like God wasn't around. Be as honest as you can be about how your faith was affected during this time, whether it was a pretty experience or not. Even at this age, your kids can hear about struggles. It makes faith more realistic to them and gives them permission to struggle without feeling guilty.

Ask your kids if they've ever had a prayer answered by God that they can remember. Again, if they don't have one, don't force it. Ideally, this won't just be you talking at your kids, but it's not helpful to guilt your kids into sharing if they don't want to. As before, if they can't remember an answered prayer, then you tell a story of a time God positively answered your prayer. This psalm in *The Message* talks about celebrating and singing at the top of our lungs, so try to mix in some exuberance if you can as you tell the story.

Here's an example of one I would tell from my life: One day my wife's coworker Julia called her and told her she was in the hospital, and it was bad. Julia had been told to call her kids to come to tell her goodbye because she was going to die, and Julia found herself terrified. My wife asked if she could come to visit her at the hospital and pray with her, and Julia said yes. So we went to visit Julia in the hospital. We talked for a few minutes about nothing really, then my wife prayed for Julia. It wasn't a special or particularly powerful prayer. She just asked God to heal Julia. The next day, my wife got a call from Julia. She was being released from the hospital because everything that was wrong with her had gone away overnight. The doctors called it a miracle, so Julia was calling to thank my wife for praying for healing. What a tremendous moment and what a powerful way for God to show up!

Ages Thirteen to Eighteen

Warn your teens as you sit down to talk that you are going to give them homework and that it might even be tough homework, but that it will be worthwhile homework that will bear good fruit in their lives. You have some homework to do before you can sit down with them though, so hold tight. I know, you didn't sign up for homework, but in this case, it's necessary if you're going to be able to convince your teens to participate.

You are going to write a personal lament to God based on a current situation where you feel like he's abandoned you or isn't as active as you'd like him to be. I know not everyone is a writer, but this isn't a poem or a book or an essay—think of it as a written prayer to God. We all pray at least once in a while, and this is just formalizing that prayer on paper. Don't feel obligated to make this an exceptionally eloquent prayer or lament to God. The whole point of you completing this exercise first is to show that it's an accessible practice and that it doesn't take someone who's necessarily gifted or "an author" to do it. But it is a very specifically formatted prayer, so let's review the elements of a lament:

- An address to God: This can be super short if you need it to be short. You're simply pointing out who you're talking to in the lament. Honestly, it can be as simple as "God." If you'd like to expand on who you believe God to be, feel free to do that as well, but you don't have to.
- A description of the complaint: In the Bible, this part of the lament psalm was nearly always very direct, and it was often in the form of a question. Why are my enemies piling on top of me right now? Why is my body breaking under illness? You don't have to format it as a question, but you also might find it helpful to do that.
- A request for God's help: Again, this can be a simple request. It doesn't have to be fancy or lengthy. "God, my mental illness tears me down. Would you lift me?" "God, my friends seem like they are too busy for me. Would you remind them that I matter in their lives, if I even do?"
- An expression of trust in God: This might be the most important part of the lament, because we express our preemptive trust in God to do his work. We thank God for something he hasn't even done yet. We believe that he will do what we ask, even though he hasn't lifted a finger yet.

To give you something more personal and less biblical, here's a lament I once wrote:

> Maker of heaven and earth, I've been having a lot of seizures lately. I have fallen down the stairs twice, and I've hit my head every day for the last two weeks. I'll be honest with you: I'm sick of this garbage. I need something to change. I know that you're not only the God of the universe but also the God of my body. Heal

me, Lord, or at least make the seizures less often. At a bare minimum, could you give me a break from smacking my head so much? I believe that you're listening right now, and I praise you for answering this prayer according to your will and purposes. Thanks for listening and I love you.

• •

Now it's your turn to write a lament. Take something real and present in your life right now and write out your prayer to God following the pattern outlined above. Once you've done that, it's time to talk with your teens. You're going to walk through Psalm 13 with them, armed with the description of laments above, and you're going to explain how laments work and why they matter. Then, you are going to share the lament you've written based on your struggles.

After that, you're going to invite them to write a lament. Make sure to tell them that you don't expect them to sit down in five minutes and finish the lament, though they're welcome to do just that if they can. Rather, you'd like them to take some time over the next week and pen their prayer to God. Then you are going to circle back with them and ask them to share their lament. Encourage them not to blow this experiment off because it's a valuable experience with God, one that can be used over and over again when things start to go sideways in life.

ENGAGING WITH YOURSELF

1. When was the last time you struggled to maintain control of your anger? If you were successful, how did you do it? If you weren't successful, what was the damage done by your anger?

2. How weird does it feel to be given permission to say prayers like David did in this psalm, where he's praying against his enemies and asking for their downfall? Does that feel outdated in today's world somehow?

3. If you were to write a lament today, what would it be about? What's keeping you from writing that lament right now?

4. Do you feel as though you've not been permitted to be honest with God about the things that are frustrating or disappointing you in your life? Why do you think that is or is not the case?

> ### Verse to Consider or Memorize
> *"Do everything without complaining and arguing, so that no one can criticize you. Live clean, innocent lives as children of God, shining like bright lights in a world full of crooked and perverse people."*
> Philippians 2:14–15

It's worth revisiting this verse simply because it is the root cause of many people thinking that laments are dangerous. But reading this in context gives us a different picture entirely. It's not that we should never complain to God about things that aren't going the way we think they ought to. This passage isn't addressing that at all. It speaks more to the whining we discussed concerning the Israelites as they wandered in the wilderness for forty years. The reason given to avoid complaining is so we cannot be criticized. Nobody will criticize us for praying, because it's a private moment between us and God. Further, part of living an innocent and clean life as a child of God is staying in close communion with God. The only way we can do this is to be brutally honest with God about the things that are disappointing or frustrating. It is intimacy with God that will cause us to shine like bright lights.

13

WE CAN PRAY BRAVELY

"Search me, O God, and know my heart;
test me and know my anxious thoughts.
Point out anything in me that offends you,
and lead me along the path of everlasting life."

Psalm 139:23–24

Engaging with the Bible

We've just finished talking about laments, which is a brave type of prayer because we let our frustrations and disappointments be made known to the creator of the universe. There is a sense in which this seems ridiculous to do, because God dwells in the heavens and we are small human beings with problems that, in the grand scheme of things, don't measure up to big-time problems. After all, we are talking about jobs and health and family, not global warming or wars or economic crises. Our problems are small, so bringing them to God at all is a form of bravery. But now we turn to a different sort of bravery in prayer, one where we ask God to search our hearts and tell us where we are lacking.

This can be a very intimidating prayer on multiple levels. For starters, we must overcome the fear of God being a thunderbolt-throwing, angry, judgmental God. So many of us have this view of God lurking in the shadows of our minds, even while we might sing songs of God's love and speak about his goodness to others. Still, we wonder if perhaps, underneath it all, God waits to send down fire from the heavens to consume everything and everyone that doesn't measure up to his standards. And God demands perfection, which means we are in trouble. We fear God largely based on biblical images of God's judgment and a poor understanding of what the sacrifice of Jesus does for us.

We see scattered throughout the Old Testament moments when God destroyed people for being unfaithful to him. The sin of Achan in Joshua 7 comes to mind. One man secretly broke the commandment of the Lord to not keep any treasures from the sacking of Jericho, and as a result, the Israelites were defeated in their next battle in Canaan. Joshua sought the Lord to understand the reason for their defeat, and the Lord revealed he was angry because someone had taken some of the treasures from Jericho for themselves. Through a series of events, it was revealed that Achan stole these items. The Lord told the Israelites to stone Achan and his family; they did this, then burned the bodies afterward.

Stories like this seem to be far too common to be ignored as we read the Bible. It's hard to not be afraid when we see such dramatic instances of judgment toward those who made mistakes. Maybe we don't want to ask God to search our hearts. Perhaps he will find some unknown wickedness there and will judge us just as harshly as he did Achan. If that's the case, maybe we're better off just letting sleeping dogs lie, so to speak. It might be better if we didn't ask God to search our hearts and cleanse us, because who knows what that cleansing will look like.

This fear is unfounded, though, due to the sacrifice of Jesus on the cross. Because we have accepted his sacrifice, God sees the righteousness of Christ when he sees us. Colossians 3:3–4 says it this way: "You died to this life, and your real life is hidden with Christ in God. And when Christ, who is your life, is revealed to the whole world, you will share in all his glory." The apostle Paul promises here that our real life is hidden with Christ in God. What a powerful promise, one that should set our minds at ease when it comes to considering the wrath of God toward any mistakes or sins we might have in our lives. Our lives being hidden with Christ means we cannot be differentiated from the righteousness of Christ in God's eyes. In other words, when God looks at us, he sees the perfection of Jesus, not our sinful self. This is precisely the nature of what took place at the cross. Jesus overcame death and the grave with his sacrifice and, therefore, restored us to a right relationship with God.

With all this in mind, we can join with the author of the book of Hebrews and boldly come to the throne of grace, asking God to search our hearts. We can ask him to test our motives without any fear of negative repercussions. Instead, he will reveal in tenderness the things we need to change, and he will challenge us to let go of our anxious thoughts. Now, letting go of anxious thoughts might seem like a tricky thing, because even though we understand today that there's a difference between worry and anxiety, this awareness wasn't around when David wrote Psalm 139, so we are left with a cry for God to know our anxieties. We understand through scientific advances now that people can have generalized anxiety disorder, which causes them to be anxious without an obvious source; people can have panic attacks, which may or may not be related to prior trauma; and people can have social anxiety, which manifests when we have to engage with others in uncomfortable ways.

I don't believe for a second that David asked God to pull these types of anxiety out of him for the simple reason that David didn't know any of these anxiety disorders existed. For this reason, I appreciate the way *The Message* paraphrase puts these verses:

> Investigate my life, O God,
> > find out everything about me;
> Cross-examine and test me,
> > get a clear picture of what I'm about;
> See for yourself whether I've done anything wrong—
> > then guide me on the road to eternal life.

Here we can more clearly see the emphasis on testing us and learning what drives us, the point of the passage. This concept echoes in 1 Thessalonians 2:4, where Paul wrote, "[God] alone examines the motives of our hearts."

But what might be the impact of asking God to investigate our lives? First Peter 1:6–7 gives some insight into the purpose of God testing us.

> There is wonderful joy ahead, even though you must endure many trials for a little while. These trials will show that your faith is genuine. It is being tested as fire tests and purifies gold—though your faith is far more precious than mere gold. So when your faith remains strong through many trials, it will bring you much praise and glory and honor on the day when Jesus Christ is revealed to the whole world.

When we invite God to investigate our motives, the result could be much the same as that of trials. Our faith will shine through and be purified. We will see the strength of our faith and will be encouraged as a result. We will be able to recognize that our faith consists of precious material and that we're precious to God. He will demonstrate his great care for us in the way he tests our hearts and our motives. Yes, there will be things that need to change, but they will come to light in love and not judgment.

So we can pray bravely and ask God to show us what needs to change, and he will be faithful to do that. More than that, he will guide us on the path to everlasting life. The key takeaway in this passage is that God won't remove us from the path to everlasting life. He won't denigrate our imperfect attempts to live well in the strength we have. He instead coaxes us into greater obedience and willingness to follow him through love and tenderness. He leads us toward everlasting life, and that is the biggest encouragement of all. We won't be abandoned to figure out the path to eternal life on our own, but God himself will show us the way, specifically and intentionally based on who we are and who God desires us to become.

Romans 8:28–29 shines some more light on what God's purposes are in purifying us: "We know that God causes everything to work together for the good of those who love God and are called according to his purpose for them. For God knew his people in advance, and he chose them to become like his Son, so that his Son would be the firstborn among many brothers and sisters." Many times, people will quote or paraphrase the first part of this passage by saying that God works everything out for good, but this unfortunately focuses on one part of the full story. We are called according to his purpose, and Paul defines that purpose as being like Jesus. We join God in accomplishing this goal when we ask him to test our motives, as that is the goal of our prayers—to become more like Jesus in our hearts and our actions.

Engaging Our Kids with This Truth

The final tool in the tenacity toolbox for our kids is centered on the idea of interacting with God so that we can learn to follow God more closely. It's good that this is the last tool because it requires a lot of the work we've already done to be accomplished for our children to pray brave prayers like this. They must know that God is for them, that God won't erupt in fierce anger toward them, and that we are hidden in Christ who is our life. Learning to pray brave prayers with open hearts toward God and how he might answer will enable our kids to grow deeper in their faith, and will give them more tenacity through stronger roots in God.

Ages Three to Seven
The best thing we can help this age group understand is what it means that our lives are hidden with Christ in God. This will give them the courage to trust God with the challenges that come their way and to pray bravely for God to draw them closer to him. To accomplish this, we will let our kids get dirty. Now, maybe you're not a parent who enjoys it when your kids get all muddy and dirty; if that's you, trust me when I say that this object lesson is worth any irritation and cleaning that might be necessary after the fact. If someone in your family has sensory issues, though, it would be best to skip this activity. See the non-muddy option listed later on instead.

    Create some mud somewhere outside for your kids to get their hands grubby in. Once you've made the mud, encourage them to dive in and make a mess. You might have a child who doesn't love getting dirty, and if that's the case, promise them they can clean up afterward, then tell them it's important this time for them to get their hands dirty. Let the kids play for a while, maybe even until they start to get a little bored. Then gather them around and tell them that they are going to present their hands for a cleanliness inspection right now, and they might even get in trouble if their hands are dirty.

Expect them to start complaining at this point about how unfair a clean inspection is. After all, you created the mud and encouraged them to play in it. Pretend to ignore all their complaints and insist that it's time for an inspection of their hands to see how clean they are. Ask them to come present their hands to you for inspection. As they bring their hands to you, cover them up with a handkerchief or a paper towel. Then tell them that their hands pass the cleanliness inspection because all you see is the clean handkerchief or paper towel.

For those families with sensory issues, here is an alternative activity that will allow you to highlight the same idea with your kids. To prepare for this idea, make sure you are wearing your most brightly colored shirt, then grab a blanket. Get your kids, then throw the blanket over your head and ask them what color your shirt is. Don't let them sneak under the blanket to see your shirt, and give them a hint that it's extra bright. Whether they guess it or can't figure it out, make sure it's a time of laughter and silliness. Then ask them why it was hard to figure out what color your shirt was. They will say something like, "Because you were under the blanket, silly!"

At the end of whichever lesson you chose, quote part of Colossians 3:3 to them, where it says we are hidden with Christ in God. Tell them that being hidden with Christ is exactly the same as having a handkerchief or paper towel over their hands for a cleanliness inspection, or having a blanket over their head. When God looks at us, he doesn't see the dirt from the mistakes we make in our lives or the color of our shirts. He doesn't see our sins at all. Instead, all he sees is the perfection of Jesus. So we don't have to worry about measuring up to what God expects of us. We already measure up through Jesus.

Ages Eight to Twelve

We are going to talk with our kids about the ancient process of smelting gold, which is purifying it using a blast furnace. Don't worry, I'm not going to ask you to suddenly become an expert on ancient smelting—that's why YouTube exists! Do a Google search for "purifying gold with a blast furnace" and look for videos. The Archimedes Channel and 911 Metallurgist have good options. Make sure you watch the video first so you'll know it will keep your kids' interest. Tell your kids that they will learn about purifying gold and how God purifies us, and then show them one of the videos. Point out that it takes extreme amounts of heat in the furnace for the gold to be purified.

Read 1 Peter 1:6–7 to them and help them understand that their faith is purified in the same way that gold is purified, by applying heat. This means that sometimes things might get uncomfortable in our lives as God purifies us. But he also promises never to leave us or forsake us, so he stays right by our side as we are being purified.

Ask your kids if they've ever felt like God has tried to purify them through difficulties and ask them to share that experience with you. If they don't have anything to share, don't push them since it's a complex question. Instead, share a time when you noticed God was purifying you through pressure. Talk about how difficult it was and how you wondered what was going on, even questioning whether God was with you through your difficulty. Then explain how in the end, you recognized the goodness of God and saw specific changes in your life because of the purification.

Read Psalm 139:23–24 from *The Message* paraphrase to them. Ask them what they think about the idea of inviting God to investigate their lives. Do they have any concerns about asking God to purify them? Point them to the promise of God's presence throughout the testing and that he will guide them on the road to eternal life.

Ages Thirteen to Eighteen

Read Psalm 139:23–24 with your teens and ask them what it might look like for God to search their hearts and test them. Entertain any answers they might have, as there's not a specific correct answer to this question. Tell them that there are at least three different ways God can search us and know our hearts and that we should pay attention to each one.

1. **The Bible.** We can know God's will by reading the Bible. In it, we read the expectations God has about how we will live our lives, the types of decisions we will make, and a definition of sorts for what it means to live righteously. Encourage your teens to start by reading the Sermon on the Mount in Matthew 5–7 to see what Jesus says about living a life pleasing to God. Suggest that they read through this sermon one section at a time and take notes about what to do and what not to do to honor God with their decisions. As they read, they have to keep in mind that God will guide them along the path to everlasting life. He will never expect them to have everything together all at once, and he won't judge them for making mistakes. He will lovingly correct them through the other avenues that we are going to discuss momentarily.
2. **Other people.** God has placed other people in our lives and theirs to be encouragers and to challenge us when we make mistakes or sin. Both the encouragement and the challenges are important parts of friendship. Ask them if they have any friends who will push them to be godlier with their decisions; if you know of some, point

them out if your teen is struggling to come up with anyone. Share how you have friends in your life who have the permission to speak challenging things to you and correct you when you go astray. Mention to them that parents, pastors, and even teachers can fill this role in their lives too.

3. **The Holy Spirit.** We see over and over again in the New Testament that the Holy Spirit guides those whose lives are submitted to Jesus. The apostle Paul allowed the Holy Spirit to show him where to go on his missionary journeys, as one example. He was prevented from going to some places and told to go to other places by the Holy Spirit. The Holy Spirit will do the same in our teens' lives if they learn to listen carefully. It can be tricky to learn what the voice of the Holy Spirit sounds like, especially with so many other voices vying for attention right now. Entire books have been written on this topic (and haven't scratched the surface), so we won't be able to do it justice in this paragraph. Remind your teens that the Holy Spirit will never contradict the Bible, that he may correct but will never condemn, and that he will always speak with unmistakable authority. Feel free to add whatever you'd like to this description as well.

Ask your teen if there are other pathways they would add to the three you just mentioned. Ask them which they feel the most comfortable with and which they struggle with the most. Ask them how you can support their growth where they feel weaker. End with a prayer: "God, thank you that you are always for us. Thank you for guiding us on the path of everlasting life. Teach us to listen for your Holy Spirit, to know your will from the Bible, and to look for and listen to trusting relationships with others. You are a good God and we love you. In the name of Jesus, amen."

ENGAGING WITH YOURSELF

1. What emotions are stirred in you when you consider asking God to search and test your heart?

2. Do you think of God as an angry God or worry that he might extinguish you if you let him see the "real you"? Is there a history of teaching behind those emotions?

3. What response do you have to the concept of being hidden in Christ with God?

4. Do you worry that your anxieties might be judged by God, and how does this chapter help you in that regard?

> ### Verse to Consider or Memorize
> *"The LORD is merciful and compassionate, slow to get angry and filled with unfailing love."*
> Psalm 145:8

This description is one of the greatest descriptions of God in the Bible. It is like what God proclaimed when he showed himself to Moses on the mountain of God. It is what was demonstrated in the generosity of Jesus upon the cross. It is a fundamental truth about the character and nature of God. God is merciful. He is compassionate. God does not get angry quickly but is very long-suffering with mistakes. His love never fails. As you consider laying your life before God for examination, and as you encourage your children to do the same, remember that this is who God is. He is a good God to the core.

CONCLUSION

We've covered a lot in this book, and it would be easy for you to feel even more overwhelmed than ever when you think about parenting. The world is more complex than ever before, and more pressures on our kids exist for them to succumb to than we experienced when we grew up. But don't lose hope.

One perspective on parenting says we need to get everything just perfect to ensure that our kids will turn out okay. There are even verses from the Bible that seem to support this idea, like Proverbs 22:6: "Direct your children onto the right path, and when they are older, they will not leave it." This verse seems to put the responsibility even for decisions that our children make as adults directly on our shoulders if read in a certain way. After all, if our kids have left the right path (whatever that is), then it must be because we didn't guide them properly.

We all worry about being the perfect parents, because that is how we can "guarantee" that our kids will turn out right. How about this for a head-scratcher though: Even Mary and Joseph made mistakes. I mean, they left their kid in Jerusalem and started to go home without even realizing it for a whole day (Luke 2:41–52). And Jesus turned out pretty okay. He wasn't so scarred from this mistake his parents made that he was incapable of pursuing his God-given mission in life. Now, we can of course pretend that it's different because this was the Son of God, but this ignores Hebrews 5:8, which says, "Even though Jesus was God's Son, he learned obedience from the things he suffered." We don't see anything in the Lukan narrative that says Jesus suffered from being left by his parents, but it wouldn't be unreasonable to think that this incident came back to haunt him from time to time. Maybe he did wonder if his parents were going to abandon him again. Regardless, we see that Jesus overcame his parents' mistakes to accomplish all God had for him. Maybe all the pressure we put on ourselves to be perfect parents isn't from God.

We have a very interesting example in Scripture on the opposite end of the spectrum with parenting as well. We know David was called a man after God's own heart, but an examination of his children leaves much to be desired. Solomon was called by God and chosen by David to be the next king. He started his kingship off well. The Bible stories tell us how he directed the building of God's temple with great enthusiasm and passion. His dedication of the temple must be one of the highlights for the nation of Israel. We read of this great event in 1 Kings 8:6–11:

> The priests carried the Ark of the LORD's Covenant into the inner sanctuary of the Temple—the Most Holy Place—and placed it beneath the wings of the cherubim. The cherubim spread their wings over the Ark, forming a canopy over the Ark and its carrying poles. These poles were so long that their ends could be seen from the Holy Place, which is in front of the Most Holy Place, but not from the outside. They are still there to this day.

Nothing was in the Ark except the two stone tablets that Moses had placed in it at Mount Sinai, where the LORD made a covenant with the people of Israel when they left the land of Egypt.

When the priests came out of the Holy Place, a thick cloud filled the Temple of the LORD. The priests could not continue their service because of the cloud, for the glorious presence of the LORD filled the Temple of the LORD.

• •

Imagine being the king who physically ushered the presence of God into the Most Holy Place because you built the temple. We also read of other great things Solomon accomplished, such as the vast amounts of wealth flowing into Israel in annual tributes from other countries. Yet we see that Solomon did not maintain his devotion to God, as indicated in 1 Kings 11:3–6:

• •

[Solomon] had 700 wives of royal birth and 300 concubines. And in fact, they did turn his heart away from the LORD.

In Solomon's old age, they turned his heart to worship other gods instead of being completely faithful to the LORD his God, as his father, David, had been. Solomon worshiped Ashtoreth, the goddess of the Sidonians, and Molech, the detestable god of the Ammonites. In this way, Solomon did what was evil in the LORD's sight; he refused to follow the LORD completely, as his father, David, had done.

• •

So this brings us to the question: Is this David's fault? Was there something in David's life that caused Solomon to fall away from God in his old age? It seems like a ridiculous question in this context, yet we assign blame to ourselves for the decisions our adult children and even adolescent children make all the time. In the same way that David wasn't responsible for the decisions Solomon made as an old man, we are not responsible for the decisions our adolescents and adult children make.

It's important to understand the purpose of a proverb. A proverb is considered a truism. A truism is something that's generally observed to be true, not something that's always positively accurate. Every proverb needs to be read in this context, and Proverbs 22:6 follows this rule. In other words, we can read it like this: It is generally (but not always) true that children follow in the faith footsteps their parents lay out for them. A proverb is a wise observation about the way life works, not a promise or a declaration from God. This is tricky because the book of Proverbs is in the Bible, so we want to assume it's always true, but we have to apply an understanding of the type of literature we're reading to our understanding of the text.

Let's continue looking at David's children to see how the man after God's own heart raised his kids, and what the fruit of their lives was. In 2 Samuel 13, we read that David had a daughter named Tamar who was very beautiful. One of his sons, Amnon, fell desperately in love with her to the degree that he became obsessed with her and became ill in his pining for her. One of his friends helped him put together a dastardly plot that resulted in Amnon being alone in his bedroom with Tamar. Once there, Amnon raped Tamar and subsequently kicked her out of his house in shame. She went to her brother Absalom's house and lived out her life as a desolate woman there, accursed because of the culture's thoughts on her situation.

What a terrible situation, and yet it's only the beginning of the story. Two years later, Absalom invited all his brothers, including Amnon, to a feast. Once everyone had been drinking for some time, Absalom commanded his men to kill Amnon in retribution for raping Tamar. Absalom then fled and stayed in hiding from David's wrath for his murder of Amnon for years. After many years, they were reconciled, but there is still more to the story.

Several years after their reconciliation, Absalom began plotting against his father, David. Over time, he slowly turned the hearts of the people of Israel against David through deceit and deception. Finally, he asked his father if he could go to Hebron to fulfill a vow he made to God, as written in 2 Samuel 15:7–8. However, instead of fulfilling a vow, Absalom had himself crowned the new king of Israel. David and his advisors had to flee Jerusalem or risk being killed by the upstart false king, and they wept as they fled. Eventually, David and Absalom engaged in battle with their armies, and Absalom was killed by Joab. David wept at the news of Absalom's death, but with a heavy heart, returned to Jerusalem to regain his kingship.

So we can see in this brief overview of David's children that they were a disaster, dysfunctional in far worse ways than we could imagine our family ever becoming. Rapes and murders and betrayals around every corner. Yet David was a man after God's own heart. Did he fail all his children as a parent? And what about Jesus's parents? They abandoned him in an enormous city in the middle of a tremendous celebration and didn't reunite with him for nearly a week, but Jesus was able to move forward without any problems. Does the role of a parent matter at all? Are we just gatekeepers for these miniature adults, people who play little to no role in their future? No surprise, but I think the exact opposite is true. I believe we have perhaps the most important role of anyone in our children's lives, no matter what their future holds for them.

David was not a perfect man, nor was he a perfect father. We can point to many instances where David missed the mark, but he was still referred to as a man after God's own heart and was still promised an eternal kingdom that was ultimately fulfilled in Jesus Christ. But he also understood how God saw him even in his imperfections. He recognized his frailties and sought to become more like God, to become a better man and a better father. We should walk in David's footsteps in this way. We need to look at our own lives and parenting failures through the eyes of God, eyes of love, grace, and compassion for us. We should look to become more like Christ day after day and stop beating ourselves up when we stumble. Because stumbling is part of being human.

Let's not forget that it was the same David who penned Psalm 139 in the first place. We don't have any indication of what prompted him to write this psalm, but it certainly could have been one of the events we just walked through. Perhaps he felt like a failure as a father when Amnon raped his daughter, and he wanted to cry out to God for his presence, judgment, and kindness. Maybe he was writing this psalm as he narrowly escaped with his life after Absalom usurped the throne. It could even be that he wrote this psalm after Absalom was killed by Joab during the battle against David's men, as a cry for justice and righteousness to be restored. We simply don't know, but it's worth revisiting these concepts as parents to consider what truth they hold for us. We can find strength and courage by walking through Psalm 139 one last time to see what promises God has for us.

God knows us intimately and still wants to be around us. We can hold fast to the truth that God knows our hearts, has examined us thoroughly, and knows everything about us. This is a powerful and life-giving truth that we would do well to hold on to as parents. When we don't quite know how to move forward with our struggling teens, God knows our heart is to see them succeed. When we're just too tired to invest much in our kids because work took it all out of us, God is still our advocate. If we're fighting old habits of behavior that we learned from our parents, God sees that our heart is to break free and become a forerunner of healthiness for our kids. It's so vital to remember that God knows everything about us and still wants to be around us.

God is paying attention to us. God has not abandoned us in our problems. He knows when we sit down, stand up, and think anything at all. He is a caring and loving God who pays attention to all that we're going through. Now for various reasons, God doesn't always engage in solving our problems, and that's a hard pill to swallow, but God is always aware of what we're going through. One thing he promises is to give us his presence through the tender touch of the Holy Spirit. John 14:16–17 holds this amazing promise from Jesus: "I will ask the Father, and he will give you another Advocate, who will never leave you. He is the Holy Spirit, who leads into all truth. The world cannot receive him, because it isn't looking for him and doesn't recognize him. But you know him, because he lives with you now and later will be in you." Jesus asked the Father to send another advocate in the Holy Spirit, and the Father answered. We're never without a divine support system, because the Holy Spirit is within us. Romans 8:26 tells us that the Holy Spirit will intercede to God on our behalf in groans too deep for words; in other words, when we don't even know what to pray, the Holy Spirit has still got our back.

God sees us. God looks at our anxious thoughts and knows they are there. God recognizes our depression and acknowledges it. God sees our bipolar episodes and accepts them at face value. There is no judgment, only being seen by God. And we are seen the same way Hagar was seen when she was running from Abram and Sarai into the wilderness with no idea of where to go. God showed up to her, gave her hope and a future for herself and her son, and told her what to do next. While we might not have an angelic visitation to point us to our next steps, we can know with certainty that God sees us and knows us fully.

God knows our words. When we lose our temper, God sees the broken heart behind the words and guides us to seek forgiveness from those we've hurt. When we allow bitterness to begin to settle into our souls, God gently but firmly points it out to us and invites us to repentance. Bitterness is a particular risk for us as parents because our kids can get into stubborn phases where they keep making the same types of mistakes over and over again. Perhaps they are letting their grades slip or perhaps it's something more serious like drug experimentation. No matter the specifics, we can let bitterness into our hearts by beginning to believe they will never change.

Hebrews 12:15 says, "Watch out that no poisonous root of bitterness grows up to trouble you, corrupting many." Two key points in this verse are worth expanding on. First, the root of bitterness becomes poisonous in that it affects everything it touches. Its corrosiveness might start with our relationship with our kids, but it will quickly expand to other parts of our lives if we don't deal with it quickly. Beyond that, the root of bitterness will corrupt many. This means that its poison will spread not only within our souls but to others as well. In the context of parenting, this might mean our kids begin to reflect our bitterness back to us, and it could even spread to their friends. The way out of bitterness can only be found through repentance, both before God and to those we have been bitter toward. This is hard work, but it will bear tremendous fruit.

God is all around and within us. We don't tend to focus on this very much most of the time. We are too busy "living our lives" to consider what God might be up to within and around us, but it's something that simply must change. Perhaps the biggest opportunity for us to model spirituality to our kids is contained in this idea. If we're consistently looking for and seeking out the presence of God in our circumstances, it will be obvious to our children. They will begin to ask questions about why we are so convinced God is among us, and this provides a chance for us to share our faith naturally. First Peter 3:15 says, "You must worship Christ as Lord of your life. And if someone asks about your hope as a believer, always be ready to explain it." Actively looking for and expecting the presence of God is one way to worship Christ as the Lord of our lives, and there is no better audience for our hope than our children.

We must develop a ritual of gratitude. Another open avenue for training our kids is this ritual of gratitude. If we are thankful even in bad seasons, our children will see that this is part of the backbone of our lives, not simply something we do when it's easy. This is different, though, than always seeing a half-empty glass as overflowing with goodness. We must be careful not to overstate our gratitude, because then it will be perceived as fake. When times are difficult, we shouldn't hide from that, but we can still find things to be grateful for. Here's a funny personal anecdote. I once told my wife that if she were a superhero, she would be Silver Lining Girl because she can find the good in any circumstance. If she were in a car crash, she would say something like, "Well, at least the car isn't totaled." Over the years, I have learned that I need more Silver Lining Girl in my life because it's often in the silver linings that we find God.

We cannot escape God. No matter where we go, God is right there with us. This is true not only because of his Holy Spirit but also because God is everywhere all at once. The key thing to remember is that our mental health struggles won't cause God to run away from us. Our depression, anxiety, bipolar, dissociative identity disorder, or whatever else we might be struggling with won't disappoint God. He doesn't view mental health conditions as sinful things to be purged from humanity. No, they are simply things that exist, like broken arms and type 1 diabetes. These things aren't anyone's fault; rather, they are results of living in a broken and complex world. In other words, we are stuck with God, even with all our frailties. The quicker we can jump into this mode of thinking, the better off we will be. This is another chance for us to bring light and life to our children, who are (statistically speaking) more likely to be dealing with depression or anxiety than not. If we can convince them that God isn't rejecting them for their struggles, this will be a major victory for the kingdom of God.

Darkness is light to God. There are times when we will want to hide in our shame or sorrow because of the things we're going through in our lives. The promise of God, excruciating as it might appear to be, is that his light and love pierce every darkness. Darkness and light are the same to God. This means we cannot run from God, but also that he will never abandon us. His commitment is to always be for us, and that is a promise that will stand the test of time.

Walking in the light of God also means being in intimate fellowship with other Christians. I'm not talking about the kind of fellowship where you share a piece of pie twice a year and act like everything is hunky-dory even when things are left unspoken and hurts remain unexamined. No, I'm talking about the type of deep, intimate friendship that has permission to say hard things to you—to ask if you're drinking again to self-medicate, to check in on your mental health, or to suggest you find some medication to help you cope better with your life. These ride-or-die friends are truly the difference between isolation and community, and the better connected you are, the better chance you have of thriving. If your kids see that you have true friendships, then they might long for that in their own lives. And that, my friends, is a beautiful thing indeed.

God knows our broken parts and still loves us. It's easy as parents to feel the pressure to have our lives together and to present a finished, perfect product to our kids, and to God. But that's not a reality, because we all have our broken parts. Here's the glorious thing about God and our children both—they aren't looking for perfection. They look at us with eyes of love, regardless of the mess that might be there, and see someone they adore. They aren't waiting for us to figure everything out and present an ideal human being. They love us with all our quirks and with all our faults and with all our idiosyncrasies because all those things are precisely what makes us, us. It's time to let go of the quest for perfection and rest instead in the knowledge that we are loved. Period. End of story. By God and by our kids.

We are extraordinary. Instead of accepting that we are somewhat broken but still functioning humans, we are called to view ourselves as truly extraordinary. This requires us to take a step back from that brokenness we are so aware of and look at the broader picture, even some of the things we can take for granted. The body functions perfectly and without flaws (mostly), and we don't even have to pay attention to a lot of it most of the time. Because our bodies function so well and so automatically, we often take them for granted. Beyond the ingenuity of our bodies, we each have specific things that are remarkable about us. For example, because I am an accountant in my day job, I have memorized about seventy-five different Microsoft Excel functions, how to use them, when to use them, and the appropriate format for each of them. You have similarly astounding things that you just know how to do because of your job, as an example. But this is about more than job skills. There are countless skills and attributes we each have that are extraordinary, and it would be obvious to us if we could sit outside ourselves and consider it. Learning to view ourselves as extraordinary is a powerful thing to model to our children too, because they have so many people and things pushing them down, telling them they are worthless. If we can teach our kids that they are extraordinary because God says so and because the facts agree, then we give them a strong weapon against those things conspiring against them.

God knows all our days. Complexities abound in this concept that God knows everything that is going to happen in our lives. On the one hand, we might understand this idea to mean we are left as robots who are perfunctorily executing what God has already ordained for us, and we have no choice in anything that matters. Sure, maybe we get to choose the color of our socks, but with the big decisions, God has already decided what we are going to do. It's hard to imagine a God who is aware of our choices yet doesn't intervene, though some take this middle ground. They say God is aware of the decisions we are going to make and has accounted for them in his records, so to speak, but doesn't intrude. There are complexities in this perspective as well; for example, at what point does God intervene, because we certainly have all had times when we pleaded for God to do something, yet it seems he did nothing instead.

Another option, the one I argue for in this book, says God is aware of all the potential outcomes of every event in history. His book, in other words, is far more complex than we might imagine. God has to learn what's in our hearts through what we do, and he sits back and allows our free will to lead the way. In some ways, this makes God appear smaller, because he is not jumping into every opportunity to demonstrate his grandeur, but there are practical considerations too. I think of the old movie *Bruce Almighty*. In this movie, Jim Carrey's character is given the power of God for a small section of the city. He is overwhelmed by all the prayer requests, so he auto-answers "yes" to every prayer request. Chaos ensues, but my favorite moment has to be when everybody wins the lottery. Unfortunately, they all won only a few dollars because the jackpot was split so many ways. This is exactly the type of trouble that would happen if God interrupted our free will with his power regularly. Our lives are too intertwined with one another to have easy answers to all the difficulties we encounter.

Our best bet in difficult theological quandaries like this question about God's eternality is to trust what we do know and what we do understand about who God is. We know he is for us, we know God will never abandon us, and we know the Holy Spirit is a guide and advocate for us. We must choose to rest in these truths, regardless of where we land on the tougher theological challenges. And we can model to our kids this combination of trusting and being confused by the intricacies of God. A good verse to talk about with our kids related to this concept is Isaiah 55:8, which says, "'My thoughts are nothing like your thoughts,' says the LORD. 'And my ways are far beyond anything you could imagine.'" It's a fascinating conversation in which to ask your kids what ways they think God's thoughts are different from ours.

We can be emotional. Even when we trust in God's character as it's revealed in the Bible, we're also permitted to express our disappointments and angry thoughts with God. A quick look through the Old Testament, and Psalms in particular, reveals that the saints of old regularly engaged God with their emotions. We even see Abraham arguing with the Lord in Genesis 18 about destroying Sodom and Gomorrah. It's difficult for many of us to even imagine arguing with God about something he plans to do or appearing to be more righteous and generous than God, but that's exactly what happened in this story. While this moment in Abraham's life isn't primarily about anger, it shows that God welcomes our engagement with him, even on major topics.

Hebrews 4:16 says, "Let us come boldly to the throne of our gracious God. There we will receive his mercy, and we will find grace to help us when we need it most." Boldness sometimes includes deep emotions, and there is no judgment found in this verse or others. No, God instead promises to give us mercy and grace. The best part of this verse is that we will receive these things when we need them the most. God will examine our hearts and supply exactly what we need precisely when we need it. While this might not defuse our anger, it does remind us of the good heart of God. So, when we find our kids struggling with their emotions about the way things are working out in a given situation, we can encourage them to express their frustration to God. We can even model this for them. It produces a healthier relationship with God—one that will last.

We can pray bravely. Perhaps the bravest prayer we can ever pray is to ask God to search our hearts for something that doesn't please him. We are inviting God to test our motives and show us where we are lacking. If we're honest with ourselves, we already know that our motives are not always pure, so it's a tough prayer. The more we can model this type of transparency to our kids, the better their relationship with God will be. One thing we should talk to our kids about is that God never asks us to fix everything at once. It would be completely overwhelming if God gave us a list of all the things that aren't quite right in our hearts and told us that we needed to get on top of all of them at once. He is a kind God who won't overwhelm us. Even better, God provides us with specific guidance through the Holy Spirit to show us how to make these changes. It's not left up to us to figure out how to be better. Helping our kids understand this is vital so they don't feel lost.

Psalm 139 is a masterpiece in many ways. David captures the very essence of what it means to walk with God. He underscores the tender care God has for us, how his omnipresence can comfort us in dark seasons, and how his omniscience supports us when we are confused. David reminds us that God is never far from us, no matter how it feels. God is ever-present, always near us, and always able to step in and provide us with the loving support we need. There is nowhere we can turn where God's presence isn't with us. These truths are powerful for building habits of tenacity in our own lives and for our children.

ACKNOWLEDGMENTS

I wrote the majority of the first draft of this book during a weeklong writing retreat in Portland, Oregon. I got away from all my typical distractions, excuses, and responsibilities. A special word of thanks goes to my wife, Barbara, for allowing me to escape all the pressure of everyday life to just write for eight days straight. It's nothing I've ever done, so neither of us knew if it would work. Well, it worked, and I'm forever grateful that Barbara gave me the space and the trust to experiment in this way.

My kids, Jonathon, Sean, Cynthia, and Elijah, were in large part my long-term guinea pigs for these ideas. While I didn't try all these ideas out exactly as they're laid out in this book, and they weren't centered on Psalm 139 at the times I did try them, my kids nevertheless are the source material for this book. I want to thank them for being my experiments, for loving me through all the mistakes we made raising them, and for trusting us enough to walk alongside us even when things got weird.

I want to give a special thank you to Lindsay and Catherine. I think I thank them in about every book I write, but that's what good friends do for you—they earn acknowledgments by loving you well. Thank you both for continuing to believe in me and encouraging me even when I worry that I am going to run out of words.

Kevin, you encouraged me to keep going with my writing journey when I was about to throw in the towel. It was your words that lent me strength when I wanted to quit, and this book exists in part because of you.

For my super-agent, Mary, thanks for always finding a home for my creative ideas. Not too long ago, I only dreamed about writing books like this. Because you believed in me and thanks to all your hard work, now my dreams are a reality. It still feels like a dream, but I'm so grateful for you and everything you do for me—including all the times I ask you random questions and you answer them anyway because we are also friends.

Thank you as well to Jason Fikes and the whole team at Leafwood Publishers. I'm so excited to see how far this book will reach. Thanks for trusting me in this project.